A MUSICAL P[...]

THE HAPPY TIME

Book by
N. RICHARD NASH

Music by
JOHN KANDER

Lyrics by
FRED EBB

Based upon the Play by
SAMUEL A. TAYLOR

And the book by
ROBERT L. FONTAINE

Original Production Directed and Choreographed by
GOWER CHAMPION

Produced on the New York Stage by
DAVID MERRICK

THE DRAMATIC PUBLISHING COMPANY

CHICAGO

THE HAPPY TIME
A Musical Play in Two Acts
For Seven Men and Twelve Women

CHARACTERS

JACQUES BONNARD . . . . *a photographer*

PHILIPPE . . . . *his brother*

SUZANNE . . . . *Philippe's wife*

BIBI . . . . *their son*

LOUIS . . . . *the third brother*

FELICE . . . . *his wife*

NANETTE ⎤
GILLIE ⎬ . . . . *their daughters*
ANNABELLE ⎦

GRANDPERE . . . . *the patriarch*

BELLA ⎤
SYLVIE ⎪
LIZETTE ⎬ . . . . *"The Six Angels"*
MONIQUE ⎪
DORINE ⎪
GRACE ⎦

LAURIE MANNON . . . . *a teacher*

FOUFIE ⎤ . . . . *Bibi's schoolmates*
GANACHE ⎦

Dancers and Singers

PLACE: *Jacques Bonnard's studio, and in St. Pierre, a small town in Canada.*

TIME: *The present.*

3

SYNOPSIS OF SCENES AND SONGS

ACT ONE

Scene One: Jacques' Studio.
"The Happy Time" . . . . Jacques

Scene Two: The Bonnard home.
"He's Back . . . . Bonnard family

Scene Three: The theatre.
"Catch My Garter". . . . . . . The Six Angels
"Tomorrow Morning" . . . Jacques, Grandpere,
Bibi and The Six Angels

Scene Four: Bibi's bedroom.
"Please Stay". . . . . Bibi
"I Don't Remember You" . . . . Jacques

Scene Five: The Classroom.
"St. Pierre" . . . . . . Laurie and Schoolboys
"I Don't Remember You" (Reprise) . . . Laurie
and Jacques

Scene Six: The School yard.
"Without Me" . . . . Bibi and
Schoolmates

Scene Seven: The Bonnard garden.
"The Happy Time" (Reprise) . . . . . Jacques

ACT TWO

ACT ONE

SCENE: A photographer's studio--a bare stage with
a large projection screen in the background and
a light stand or spotlight near C.)

AT RISE OF CURTAIN: JACQUES BONNARD, the
photographer, enters. He goes about his work,
setting up his lights so they will focus on a pedestal. Now he selects the object he is to photo-
graph--a rose. He places it, in and out of a
vase, trying to discover which way is best, then
readjusts his lights. Now, the camera: frame,
focus, opening, speed. He is ready to shoot.)

(Click! The screen comes alive with a picture of the
rose, in color; a small area of the screen. *Click,
click, click, click!* A series of shots of the rose:
varying views, varying placements on the screen.
Then suddenly--the rose appears--unaccountably!
--in a woman's hand!* He stops. *Wha that?*
The picture fades to black. *Click!* The screen
comes alive with a picture of the rose--by itself--
exactly as he is shooting it. He is relieved. He
smiles a little. He thinks: *There it goes, my
imagination again, imagining that the rose was in
a lady's hand. Click!* There! again! But this
time the rose isn't in a lady's hand--it's in the
lapel of a man's suit coat! *Click!)*

(JACQUES is himself troubled. He has to get rid of
this image. Insinuating into Jacques' subconscious
now--and faintly heard by us--the Memory Music

*This can also be done by using a spotlight to give a brief glimpse of
the actor playing the role, posing as indicated in the stage direction.

7

which preludes THE HAPPY TIME. During
this, JACQUES is now surrendering to--what?
Is it memory? . . . is it now? On the screen
we now see the face of GRANDPERE, smelling
the rose in his lapel. Suddenly the picture is
renegade! It breaks into a number of pieces,
jumps about, reassembles! Other faces, other
flowers or a very rapid series of pictures, each
being shown just barely long enough to be seen.
Gone! The screen goes to black.)

JACQUES (a wry smile on his face, half annoyed,
   half amused)
You know, it's a very strange thing. The memory plays tricks . . . You see, every time I
take a picture of this rose, it reminds me of
something else.
  (Suddenly the memory intrudes. Grandpere's face appears C, then a huge birthday
  cake with many candles--laughter, move-
  ment, the half-seen gaiety of a half-remem-
  bered birthday party. There is a huge, glow-
  ing picture of the man and the cake: GRAND-
  PERE about to blow the candles out, a laughing face, full of joy and mischief.)

JACQUES
Something--another place--somebody--long ago!
Whatever is wrong with me, I do not know.
In the old days when I would feel this way--
quickly!--I would go home! . . .
But, now . . .. where is home?
  (A wry shrug.)
Perhaps home is only in my memory.

(MUSIC)

A memory of a small-town name--
St. Pierre, in French Canada.

(On the screen: A picture of the entire
BONNARD FAMILY, seated for dinner.
Like all the pictures heretofore, this
one is in the lush, over-romanticized
color that happy memories make.)

(The BONNARD FAMILY now starts to appear on the
stage. PHILIPPE and SUZANNE first, then
their teen-age son, BIBI. Then LOUIS and
FELICE BONNARD appear with their three
teen-age daughters, NANETTE, GILLIE and
ANNABELLE. Finally comes GRANDPERE,
as dapper as always, waxed mustache and all.
They prepare for dinner.)

JACQUES (sung)
REMEMBER A DRAFTY HOUSE WITH ROOMS
TO SPARE
THOSE SUNDAYS----

SUZANNE (spoken, to her husband, PHILIPPE)
Is your brother there? The potage will get
ice cold if they do not hurry!

JACQUES
REMEMBER THE NAPKIN RING, THE DINNER
PLATE
A POCKET WATCH----

PHILIPPE (looking at his watch)
They're late! They're late! Bibi! Call
your uncle!

BIBI (calling)
Uncle Louis! Aunt Felice!

JACQUES
REMEMBER THE CHILD, THE BOY,
THE VOICE IN THE HALL!

(LOUIS and FELICE enter with their daughters.)

LOUIS
    I'm sorry I'm late. I have to wait for my four
    women!

JACQUES
    REMEMBER THE MEAN OLD MAN,
    BUT MAYBE THE YOUNGEST OF US ALL.

(GRANDPERE enters, a flower in hand.)

GRANDPERE (suddenly)
    Louis--you thief! What have you done with
    my pictures? Thief!

LOUIS
    Pictures? Who stole your stupid naked pictures,
    you old goat?

        (Romantic color picture of the family
        enlarges and will ultimately go out
        of focus and disappear. Meanwhile:)

JACQUES (spoken)
    There they are, my family. My brother Louis,
    who drinks; his wife Felice, who is the reason;
    and their three charming daughters who are the
    result. And here is my brother Philippe, mana-
    ger and musical director of St. Pierre's only
    vaudeville theatre; his wife Suzanne and her son
    Bibi, my godson. I taught him how to fly a kite,
    how to play poker, at the age of four. Important
    things like that. --Will you look at that boy?
    Grown a foot since I saw him. First thing his
    Uncle Jacques does is get him some long pants.
    And here's my father. He always called me his
    idiot boy. Why the idiot? Well, what else would
    you call a boy who runs away from home at six-
    teen to become a photographer?

You should have heard him. "A son of mine going around the country with a pony, making children say 'cheese.'" And you know what? Even after all my prizes and exhibitions, he would always greet me the same way. "Ah, look who's here--the idiot boy. How's the pony?"

(Music)

Maybe -- was he right? I don't know.
    (Sings)
HOW NICE IF THE SIGHT OF THEM SHOULD
    MAKE YOU LAUGH
WHILE I ENLARGE THE PHOTOGRAPH
REMEMBERING, REMEMBERING,
THE HAPPY TIME.
    (To family.)
Hold it!

SUZANNE
    Jacques!
        (The family ad lib general greetings.)

GRANDPERE
    Ah, look who's here! My idiot boy.
        (They embrace. Then:)
    How's the pony?
        (Family sits.)

JACQUES
    Is that the way you welcome your favorite son, Papa?

GRANDPERE
    Welcome, my favorite son. When are you leaving?

JACQUES
    Soon, Papa. Don't worry.

13

BIBI
  I wish you would stay forever!

JACQUES
  Well, at least there is one Bonnard who really
  welcomes me. And he shall be rewarded . . .
  with a pair of long pants!

BIBI
  Uncle Jacques!

PHILIPPE
  That is very generous of you, Jacques, but there
  is nothing wrong with Bibi's pants. They are
  brand new . . .

JACQUES
  But they are for a boy, a child! My godson is a
  man. Long pants.

SUZANNE
  All the boys in Bibi's class wear the same thing,
  Jacques. Mademoiselle Mannon feels that until
  they are in their senior year . . .

JACQUES
  Who is this Mademoiselle Mannon who has the
  right to tell my godson how to dress? Some
  crabbed old maid who doesn't want a man to
  look like a man! No, Bibi shall have long pants
  and what's more . . . an evening out with his
  Uncle Jacques! There is an act at your theatre,
  Philippe . . . The Six Angels. . . . They are
  acrobats. I know them well, one in particular
  . . . and tonight I shall present Bibi!

PHILIPPE
  I am sorry, Jacques, but Bibi is not permitted
  to go backstage. Both Suzanne and I feel that . . .

14

JACQUES
What? You are the musical director of the theatre
and your own son has never been backstage? You
want to make a cripple out of him? Bibi! Tonight! The Six Angels!

GRANDPERE
Me, too! I come, too!

JACQUES
Who said you? Bibi, get ready!

PHILIPPE
Come now, Jacques, I mean it. Besides, he
has school tomorrow.

JACQUES
Well, I mean it, too. If the boy has his heart
set on going to the vaudeville . . .

PHILIPPE
. . . Of course he wants to go, and if he does
go, I will not try to stop him.

JACQUES
Good! It is settled! Come on, Bibi.

PHILIPPE
He will stop himself. You may not know this,
Jacques, but Bibi has become a boy of some
responsibility.

JACQUES
Bibi, you want to go?

BIBI
Yes, I do, but . . .

JACQUES
You mean you will not?

15

BIBI
  I . . . thank you, Uncle Jacques.

JACQUES
  Eh, assassin! What did you do to my godson?
  I left him in your care. He was a nice healthy
  little devil--full of hell! What did you do--beat
  him?

PHILIPPE
  Not a bit! Never have I laid an angry hand on
  this boy! It is true, Bibi?

BIBI
  It is true, Papa.

JACQUES
  Well, I have!
      (They start to spar, and in the midst
      of it:)
  Eh! What is your favorite color tie?

BIBI
  Red, yellow, and blue!

JACQUES
  Good! I have a thousand of them for you! And
  a new hat, and presents for everybody! Come
  on, help me unpack!
      (He rises.)

SUZANNE
  Wait! Not now! Dinner is on the table!

BIBI
  Mama, he has some ties for me!

PHILIPPE
  After dinner, Bibi!

JACQUES
    It will only take a minute! Come on!
        (JACQUES and BIBI depart.)

PHILIPPE (calling after them)
    No, Jacques! Wait a minute!

SUZANNE
    The dinner! What about my dinner?

GRANDPERE
    Well . . . you can choose your friends . . .

        (SONG: "HE'S BACK")

GRANDPERE (singing)
    HE'S BACK! HE'S BACK!
    MY LOVABLE PRODIGAL'S HOME AGAIN OUT
        OF THE BLUE.
    IT'S ODD! SO ODD!
    I WOKE UP THIS MORNING AWARE A DISASTER
        WAS DUE!

PHILIPPE
    HE'S BACK!

GRANDPERE
    HE'S BACK!

PHILIPPE
    I FEEL A FAMILIAR ANXIETY QUICKEN MY
        HEART.

GRANDPERE and PHILIPPE
    IF MEMORY SERVES, HE'LL SHATTER THE
        NERVES
    WE'LL WAIT AND WE'LL WONDER, WHEN
        WILL THE CALAMITY START!

PHILIPPE and LOUIS
JACQUES IS HOME
   AGAIN
BACK IN TOWN
JACQUES IS HOME
AND HOME IS UP-
   SIDE DOWN.

LOUIS
JACQUES WALKED IN
   AGAIN
CALM AND STRONG.

PHILLIPPE and LOUIS
OH, BROTHER DEAR,
   WE'RE GLAD
YOU'RE HERE
BUT DON'T STAY LONG!

GRANDPERE
HE'S BACK! HE'S BACK!
MY LOVABLE PRODI-
   GAL'S HOME AGAIN
OUT OF THE BLUE.
IT'S ODD! SO ODD!
I WOKE UP THIS MORN-
   ING
AWARE A DISASTER
   WAS DUE.

HE'S BACK! HE'S BACK!
I FEEL A FAMILIAR
   ANXIETY
QUICKEN MY HEART.
IF MEMORY SERVES
   HE'LL
SHATTER THE NERVES,
WE'LL WAIT AND WE'LL
   WONDER
WHEN WILL THE CA-
   LAMITY START!

SUZANNE and FELICE
NOT THAT THERE'S NOT A WARM AFFECTION
FLOWING IN EVERY BREAST.
WE NEED HIM, WE KNOW, BUT EVEN SO
WE NEED OUR REST.

NOT THAT WE AREN'T GLAD TO SEE HIM,
NOT THAT HE ISN'T DEAR.
BUT THREE LITTLE WORDS FOR TROUBLE'S
COMING

SUZANNE, FELICE and NANETTE
THREE LITTLE WORDS THAT SPELL MIS-
FORTUNE

SUZANNE, FELICE, NANETTE and GILLIE
THREE LITTLE WORDS TO MAKE YOU SHAKE
ARE

18

SUZANNE, FELICE, NANETTE, GILLIE AND
  ANNABELLE
    "JACQUES IS HERE!"
    NOT THAT THERE'S NOT A WARM AFFECTION
    FLOWING IN EVERY BREAST.
    WE NEED HIM, WE KNOW, BUT EVEN SO
    WE NEED OUR REST.

    NOT THAT WE AREN'T GLAD TO SEE HIM,
    NOT THAT HE ISN'T DEAR.
    BUT THREE LITTLE WORDS TO
    MAKE YOU SHAKE ARE
    "JACQUES IS HERE!"

PHILIPPE and LOUIE   GRANDPERE
    (Sung Simultaneously with above)
    JACQUES WALKED IN   HE'S BACK! HE'S BACK!
      AGAIN   I FEEL A FAMILIAR
    CALM AND STRONG   ANXIETY QUICKEN
    OH, BROTHER DEAR,   MY HEART
    WE'RE GLAD YOU'RE   IF MEMORY SERVES
      HERE   HE'LL SHATTER
    BUT DON'T STAY LONG!   THE NERVES,
                            WE'LL WAIT AND WE'LL
                              WONDER
                            WHEN WILL THE CA-
                              LAMITY START!

ALL
    JACQUES IS HERE! JACQUES IS HERE!
    HE'S HOME! HE'S HOME!
    WE'RE TERRIBLY HAPPY TO SEE HIM, AS
      EVERYONE KNOWS.
    HE'S HOME! HE'S HOME!
    WE'LL PROBABLY NEED A VACATION
    THE MINUTE HE GOES!
    NOT THAT THERE'S NOT A WARM AFFECTION
    FLOWING IN EVERY BREAST.
    WE NEED HIM, WE KNOW,

BUT EVEN SO WE NEED OUR REST!
NOT THAT WE AREN'T GLAD TO SEE HIM
NOT THAT HE ISN'T DEAR

LOUIS and NANETTE
BUT THREE LITTLE WORDS FOR TROUBLE'S
COMING

FELICE, GILLIE and ANNABELLE
THREE LITTLE WORDS THAT SPELL MIS-
FORTUNE

GRANDPERE, SUZANNE and PHILIPPE
THREE LITTLE WORDS TO MAKE YOU SHAKE
ARE

ALL
"JACQUES IS HERE!"

(MUSIC)

PHILIPPE
Bon dieu! I'm late!

(MUSIC)

GRANDPERE
Are you sure I can't go with you?

PHILIPPE
You stay away from those Six Angels.

(MUSIC)

GRANDPERE
I feel a draft in here. . . .

(MUSIC)
20

SUZANNE
>I am so glad my son has nothing to do with those hussies!

GRANDPERE (as he follows SUZANNE and the others offstage; they take the table and chairs with them off L.)
>Hussies? They are angels out of heaven!

(Music goes directly into "CATCH MY GARTER." From the opposite side The SIX ANGELS enter in dancing costume, singing.)

>(SONG: "CATCH MY GARTER")

THE SIX ANGELS
>LOOK THERE! IT'S GASTON.
>HERE, CATCH MY GARTER,
>I HAVEN'T SEEN YOU IN AN AGE.
>
>FRANCOIS AND HENRI,
>HERE, CATCH MY GARTER,
>I BET YOU DIDN'T EVEN KNOW THAT I WENT ON THE STAGE.
>
>I COME OUT EACH EVENING
>AND TOSS MY GARTER.
>THE GENTLEMEN ADMIRE THAT A LOT.
>
>IT SAYS IN THE PROGRAM
>THAT I'M AN ANGEL
>BUT FELLOWS,
>DON'T WORRY, I'M NOT.
>
>
>THE MISTER WHO HAPPENS
>TO CATCH MY GARTER
>CAN ROLL IT UP MY LEG UNTIL IT'S TIGHT.

21

FOR THOUGH IN THE PROGRAM
IT SAYS WE'RE ANGELS
WE'RE FULL OF THE DEVIL TONIGHT.

BELLA
    Jacques! He's here!

OTHER "ANGELS"
    Where?--where? <u>where</u>!

(JACQUES strolls on stage from L. From R a
    folding screen, a bench and door are brought
    just into view.)

JACQUES
    <u>Here</u>! My little gypsies . . .

THE SIX ANGELS
    Jacques! . . . How are you! . . . Hello, Jacques!
    . . . etc.

JACQUES
    Hello, Bella. How are you?

BELLA
    In Buffalo I heard a rumor you were married!

JACQUES
    In Pittsburgh I heard the same rumor!

BELLA
    How's your father?

SYLVIE
    How's that boy?

JACQUES
    That boy--they are making of him a public ac-
    countant! Time to put the cat out, time to
    scratch----

(BIBI peers around wing.)

JACQUES
Eh!--who's that? Bibi--is that you? Your father let you come after all?

BIBI
Oh, no, he didn't! I sneaked away.

JACQUES
What did you see--the show?

BIBI
Yes! And you better not tell him because----

LIZETTE
So this is Bibi! Hello, Bibi!

BIBI (his voice cracking)
Hello!

THE GIRLS (crowding around him)
Oh, look at that smile! Smile again, Bibi! . . . Oh, he's cute! . . . How old are you, little boy? . . . I certainly like your hat!

JACQUES
Easy--take it easy, girls! Bibi, this is Lizette--she walks on her head better than on her feet. This is Sylvie. Say *"Bonsoir,"* Sylvie.

SYLVIE
Bonsoir! (She goes behind screen.)

BIBI (buttoning her)
Oh, if my father could see me now!

PHILIPPE (calling from offstage)
    Bella!

BIBI
    Papa!

PHILIPPE (offstage)
    May I have a word with you?

JACQUES
    Vite!--behind the screen!

(BIBI rushes behind the screen, not knowing
    SYLVIE is undressing behind it. As if
    catapulted, he's out again. SYLVIE'S
    head appears above the screen, then
    ducks down again.)

PHILLIPE (offstage)
    Bella!

BIBI
    She is naked!

JACQUES
    Bibi--whatever is behind there will never hurt
    you! Go back!

BIBI
    No! I can't.

JACQUES
    Bibi--you have two choices! You go behind and
    close up your eyes--or you go behind and keep
    them open! And I beg you--for the sake of the
    family name--keep your eyes open!

        (BIBI runs behind screen again.)

            (PHILIPPE enters)
            24

PHILLIPE
    Forgive me, Bella, I will only be----Oh. *Bonsoir*,
    Jacques.

JACQUES
    Bonsoir, bonsoir, Philippe!

PHILIPPE
    I will only be a minute, Bella. Your act goes
    better tonight, yes?
        (He takes out the heavy watch JACQUES
        spoke of.)
    You save two whole minutes only in tempo. Two
    minutes is very much.

JACQUES
    Oh, two minutes is a lot. If you save two minutes
    every year, when you are seventy years old, you
    will have two extra hours to be sick.

PHILIPPE
    Thank you, Jacques. Now, if you can take out
    two minutes tomorrow night as well--better--
    much better. You come home, Jacques?

JACQUES
    Not yet. I think I will take the girls----We will
    make a little allez-oop . . .
        (Ad Libs.)
    You will come with us?

PHILLIPE
    No, thank you. One member of the family
    Bonnard making the allez-oop is more than
    enough! *Au'voir--au'voir!*

(The instant PHILIPPE goes, SYLVIE raises her head.)

SYLVIE
    Jacques--hurry up!--help!

MONIQUE
>He fainted!
>>(MONIQUE pulls the screen away. BIBI
>>can be seen. He is half-out.)

ALL
>Bibi! Give him air! . . . No--brandy! . . .
>Rub his wrists!

JACQUES
>Brandy! Give him a little brandy!

LIZETTE
>Here it is!

JACQUES
>Stand back! Open your mouth, boy--it is
>brandy. . . . He must be happy, he's smiling.

BELLA
>I'll hold his head.

JACQUES
>Bibi! Bibi, *mon petit, mon garcon!* --you are all
>right?

BIBI
>Yes--I think so--yes.

JACQUES
>Give him a little air. Breathe, boy! Oh, *merde*,
>the boy does not even know how to breathe!
>Breathe, *stupide!*

BIBI (breathing; indicating LIZETTE)
>What is that perfume! . . . Did you say Paris?

(MUSIC)

JACQUES
That is the brandy you are smelling.

LIZETTE
Give him a little more.

JACQUES
No, no, enough! He has never had brandy!

BIBI
Oh, yes, I have! Grandpere's chocolates have brandy centers!

(MUSIC)

(All laugh. BIBI takes the bottle and has another swig. He laughs triumphantly.)

BIBI
He did not know I was here, did he?

JACQUES
No! He did not--and better he should not! Go home!

BIBI
No--not yet!

JACQUES
You have to wake up early and go to school! If I keep you out late tonight, what will you do in the morning?

BIBI
What will you do?

JACQUES

Eh bien! Me?

27

(He sings "TOMORROW MORNING". He is soon joined by BIBI and THE SIX ANGELS. Doing the song, each of the SIX ANGELS, one by one, goes behind the screen. Each reappears, the other side of the screen, fully clothed. The last and prettiest of the Angels comes from behind the screen with -- GRAND-PERE!)

(SONG: "TOMORROW MORNING")

JACQUES
    OH! TOMORROW MORNING THE SUN WILL
        SHINE
    WITH A BUD AWAKENING ON EVERY VINE
    AND THE LEAVES WILL TREMBLE
    AND THE BIRDS WILL PEEP
    AND TOMORROW MORNING
    I'LL SLEEP!

    TOMORROW MORNING I'LL DO MY BEST
    TO ENJOY THE MORNING IN A GOOD NIGHT'S
        REST,
    BUT THIS EVENING'S CELEBRATION
    JUST WON'T KEEP
    SO TOMORROW MORNING
    I'LL SLEEP!

    THERE'S A BRIGHT BLUE STAR
    AND I'M WHERE YOU ARE
    IT'S A TRUE BONSOIR,
    NOT TO STAY AWAKE
    WOULD BE A LARGE MISTAKE.

JACQUES   SIX ANGELS

  IF THE WINE IS HEADY
  AND THE LIGHTS ARE   IF THE WINE IS HEADY
    LOW   AND THE LIGHTS ARE
  THEN MY ARM IS READY   LOW,
    AND   THEN MY ARM IS READY
  I'M SET TO GO,   AND I'M SET TO GO,
  IT'S A WASTE OF MOON-
    LIGHT
  TO BE COUNTING SHEEP
  AND TOMORROW MORNING
  IS TIME ENOUGH TO

BIBI

    TOMORROW MORNING THE SUN WILL SHINE
    WITH THE BUDS AWAKENING ON EVERY VINE
    AND THE BREEZE WILL WHISTLE
    AND THE BROOK RUN COOL
    AND TOMORROW MORNING

JACQUES and BIBI
    SCHOOL!

BIBI

    TOMORROW MORNING I'LL DO MY BEST
    TO EMPLOY MY CLASSROOM FOR A GOOD
      NIGHT'S REST
    BUT TONIGHT I'M FLYING AND MY HEAD
      IS SWELLED
    THOUGH TOMORROW MORNING

JACQUES and BIBI
    EXPELLED!

    THERE'S A BRIGHT BLUE STAR
    AND I'M WHERE YOU ARE
    IT'S A TRUE BONSOIR

(Enter GRANDPERE.)

GRANDPERE
  NOT TO STAY AWAKE
  WOULD BE A LARGE MISTAKE.

  (ORCHESTRA CONTINUES DURING DIALOGUE)

BIBI (spoken)
  Grandpere, you saw the performance also?

JACQUES (spoken)
  Ah, you old goat, you couldn't stay away!

GRANDPERE (spoken)
  Who could stay away from six such beautiful
  ones as these?
    (Sings.)
  IT'S A WASTE OF MOONLIGHT TO BE COUNT-
    ING SHEEP.

BIBI
  BUT TOMORROW MORNING?

JACQUES (spoken)
  Forget tomorrow morning!

(DANCE INTERLUDE. An acrobatic and kick routine
  featuring the SIX ANGELS.)

ALL
  NOT TO STAY AWAKE
  WOULD BE A LARGE MISTAKE.

  (ORCHESTRA and DANCE INTERLUDE)

ALL
  BUT TOMORROW MORNING WE'LL SLEEP!

(The song concludes with JACQUES,
GRANDPERE and BIBI, like three
happy drunken sailors, on their way
home from a night on the town. The
screen, door, etc. are pulled off and
from the opposite side Bibi's bedroom /two small beds, a door and a
window and window bench/ comes into
view, as we lose GRANDPERE to
the darkness first; then we lose BIBI.
Only JACQUES is in the bedroom.
The room is lighted by pre-dawn light.
JACQUES looks about stealthily. He
goes back to the door. He whispers:)

JACQUES
    Eh--Bibi! Come on! Safe! Everybody is asleep
    . . . Bibi! Eh, Bibi! . . . Where in hell are you?

(BIBI sticks his head in at the open window. He is
    tight, more with happiness than with liquor.)

BIBI
    I'm here, Uncle Jacques!
        (He comes in through window, stumbles,
        falls, makes a racket.)

JACQUES
    No--silence! Eh, clumsy ox--why you come in
    through the window?

BIBI
    It is quieter that way.

JACQUES (at the door again)
    Papa--Papa--you are there? . . . What did you
    do with Grandpere?

(GRANDPERE also appears at the window.)

GRANDPERE
>Look! See where I am? . . . I will bet you did
>not think I also can climb up to the second floor.
>I bet you did not think that I also--
>>(Suddenly about to fall backward.)
>Eh--help me! Help!
>>(Music out. JACQUES rushes to grab him.)
>I cannot get my leg over!

BIBI
>We will pull him in by the head, yes?

GRANDPERE
>No! My head will come off!

JACQUES
>Here--go away----Let me!
>>(He pulls the old man in.)

GRANDPERE
>*Mille fois merci* -- but I was able to do this by
>myself.

JACQUES
>Yes--I am sure of it!

GRANDPERE (starting for the window again)
>Shall I show you?

JACQUES
>No--come back--I believe you! One night with
>the Six Angels . . .
>>(He turns to see BIBI open the door to his
>>closet, go inside and start to close the door
>>in upon himself.)
>You--where are you going?

BIBI
>I have to go to the bathroom.

JACQUES
    The bathroom is this way--down the hall, to
    the right.
        (BIBI goes out. GRANDPERE has both his
        hands to his head.)

GRANDPERE
    Too big, too big!

JACQUES
    What is too big?

GRANDPERE
    My head. Tomorrow always comes too soon.

JACQUES
    Go to bed, Papa.

GRANDPERE
    I hope his tomorrow will not come too soon.

JACQUES (sitting on bed)
    The sooner the better, Papa.

GRANDPERE (quietly)
    Do not ruin him, Jacques.

JACQUES
    Me?

GRANDPERE
    You. I would like him to turn into a nice,
    sensible man, like his father. Not an idiot,
    like you.

JACQUES
    Well, Papa--you have lived with him--in the
    same house--all his life! Would you say that
    you had ruined him?

33

GRANDPERE (with a little smile)
Me? No. But who am I? I am only the silly old man who lives on the third floor and looks at the pictures of naked girls and eats chocolates with brandy centers. But you! You are The Wonder Man who comes in from the Great Wide World! Every word you say--he will listen! And if you raise your hand and point--no matter what direction--that way he will go!

JACQUES
Which direction shall I point, Papa?

GRANDPERE
It might be better not to point at all! Why did you come home, Jacques?

JACQUES (picking up camera)
Don't move, Papa! Stay like that.

GRANDPERE
You have never taken so many pictures here at home! Why this time?

JACQUES
I would go anywhere for the perfect picture!

GRANDPERE
Then why here--you have a whole world to find a perfect picture.

JACQUES (the thought drives home)
Yes, perhaps. The world is a very big place.

GRANDPERE
Are you happy in it?

JACQUES
Oh, yes! Altogether, Papa!

34

(Continuing, rhapsodically.)
Oh, it's a great life, Papa! Would you believe
it? Last month I was in Calcutta . . . I took the
picture of the Ranee of Mukharata--she is the
richest woman in the world--she has false eye-
lashes made out of little sparkling black dia-
monds--it makes her cross-eyed! On Monday of
last week I was at La Scala in Milano--and I took
the picture of the most voluptuous young soprano.
In the evening I went back to my hotel . . . there
was a knock at the door and I opened my door
and----

GRANDPERE (with a flash of irritation)
    Stop it! Why do you pretend to be a fool?

JACQUES
    What?

GRANDPERE
    Stop pretending to be a fool!

JACQUES
    Why do you disapprove of me?
        (The argument comes to a stop.
        GRANDPERE feels perhaps he has
        cut too deeply.)

GRANDPERE
    I . . . disapprove of all my children.

JACQUES
    No, you don't! I have never heard you say a
    single disapproving word to Philippe! And even
    Louis--the night he was married--you said to
    him "You did that very well, my son!" What did
    he do so well? She was four months pregnant!

GRANDPERE
You get married--pregnant or not--and I will say the same to you.

JACQUES
Papa--tell me--don't I do anything very well?

GRANDPERE
Ah, yes, you take pictures very well. And you have shown me a lovely evening. You always do. Good night, Jacques.

JACQUES
Good night, Papa.

(BIBI reappears.)

BIBI
Good night, Grandpere.

GRANDPERE
Good night, Bibi. Sleep well, boy.
(GRANDPERE goes out.)

BIBI
Uncle Jacques--I have just looked at myself in the mirror and the way I look--I am not different, I am the same.

JACQUES
So?

BIBI
I--well--I don't feel the same. Uncle Jacques, am I drunk?

JACQUES
You're drunk enough. You'd better go to bed.

BIBI

Oh, no! Tonight I do not intend to sleep at all!
(Sings)
AND TOMORROW MORNING IS TIME ENOUGH
. . .

JACQUES

Shut up and get to bed!

BIBI

Oh, I wish I did not have to go to school tomorrow!

JACQUES

What? You do not like Laurie Mannon?

BIBI

Oh, I like her! It's those guys in my class,
like Ganache! Just because he's two or three
years older than I am, he thinks he knows
everything!
(Then, mournfully.)
And he does!

JACQUES

He knows everything? About what?
(As BIBI pretends to be busy.)
Hey, Bibi, what do they teach you at this boys'
school?

BIBI

I know what you mean . . . you mean hygiene, *non?*

JACQUES

Hygiene, *oui.*

BIBI

Well, we're starting with the brain and we're
working downward. We got as far as the kidneys.

JACQUES
   That's a hell of a place to stop!

BIBI
   You're thinking about love, yes, Uncle Jacques?

JACQUES (smiling)
   Yes, Bibi, I am always thinking about love!

BIBI
   Oh, so am I! What I mean is . . . Uncle Jacques,
   do you want to hear something terrible?

JACQUES
   What?

(SONG: "PLEASE STAY")

BIBI
   WHEN I WAS, I DON'T KNOW,
   MANY, MANY YEARS AGO,
   I USED TO SAY, "I LOVE YOU" TO EVERY-
      THING!
   LIKE A GAME SOMEONE PLAYS
   IT BECAME MY FAVORITE PHRASE
   AND I WOULD SAY, "I LOVE YOU" TO
      EVERYTHING!

   I LOVE YOU, MAMA,
   I LOVE YOU, PAPA
   I LOVE YOU, GRANDPERE,
   I LOVE YOU, DOG.
   I LOVE YOU, PICTURE,
   I LOVE YOU, WINDOW,
   I LOVE YOU, BED, AND
   I LOVE YOU, DOOR.
   BUT I DON'T SAY "I LOVE YOU" ANY MORE.

ISN'T THAT FUNNY, UNCLE JACQUES?
I MEAN TERRIBLE, UNCLE JACQUES?
THE SADDEST STORY YOU WERE EVER TOLD:
I HAVEN'T SAID "I LOVE YOU"
TO ANYTHING AT ALL
SINCE I WAS NINE OR TEN YEARS OLD. . . .

JACQUES
    I'm sorry to hear it, my boy.

BIBI
    Uncle Jacques, could you, I mean, would you
    stay in St.Pierre?

JACQUES
    You mean live here?

BIBI
    Yes . . . you could open up a studio. We need a
    good photographer here. Would you stay?

JACQUES
    No, Bibi.

BIBI
    I didn't think you would. I know how you feel
    about it. I mean with London and Paris and
    Lisbon and Venice--why would anybody want to
    stay in St. Pierre?
      (Sings:)
I READ A BOOK ON LONDON,
IT'S BEAUTIFUL I KNOW,
SUCH FUN TO BE IN LONDON: DON'T GO. . . .

AND LISBON MUST BE PRETTY
AROUND THIS TIME OF YEAR,
JUST MARVELOUS IN LISBON: STAY HERE.

AND VENICE TAKES YOUR BREATH AWAY,
THEY SAY . . . STAY!

IT'S DUMB TO BE IN ST. PIERRE WHEN YOU
    COULD BE IN ROME:
PLEASE STAY HOME!

VIENNA, SO YOU TELL ME,
IS JUST YOUR KIND OF TOWN,
ROMANTIC OLD VIENNA: SIT DOWN!
AND PARIS HAS THE FOUNTAINS,
THE CHURCHES AND THE LOUVRE,
SO EVERYONE LOVES PARIS: DON'T MOVE!

IN HONG KONG ORIENTAL SPLENDORS WAIT:
WAIT!

EACH NIGHT IN NEW YORK CITY IS A LOT LIKE
    NEW YEAR'S EVE
PLEASE DON'T LEAVE!
I KNOW YOU'LL NEVER DO IT, BUT I'M ASK-
    ING ANYWAY,
PLEASE PLEASE
STAY

JACQUES
    No, Bibi. Now go to sleep.

BIBI
    It's not the brandy that made tonight so beautiful.
    It was just beautiful, that's all.

JACQUES
    What are you laughing about?

BIBI
    Behind the screen!

JACQUES
    Behind the screen. . . . Did you look?

BIBI
    I . . . peeked a little.

40

JACQUES

>   Thank God! There is some hope left in the
>   world!

BIBI (singing)

>   ISN'T IT FUNNY, UNCLE JACQUES
>   I MEAN TERRIBLE, UNCLE JACQUES
>   THE SADDEST STORY THAT YOU EVER KNEW:
>   I HAVEN'T SAID "I LOVE YOU"
>   IN ALL THESE MANY YEARS . . .
>> (Speaks.)
>   But, Uncle Jacques . . . ?

JACQUES

>   Yes?

BIBI

>   I love you.
>> (The boy turns over, ostensibly to sleep.
>> JACQUES, absorbed in troubled contempla-
>> tion, comes down to speak to audience:)

JACQUES

>   Stay? Would I think to stay? Ah, no! A man
>   leaves his home, he leaves his home! *C'est ca!*
>   Then why did I come back? What was I looking
>   for? The perfect picture? A place--a dream?
>   Someone? Someone . . .

>> (Suddenly, unexpectedly a picture of LAURIE
>> is projected on the cyclorama. The girl with
>> the bicycle. JACQUES is surprised--upset--
>> by the picture. He tries to exorcise himself
>> of the memory of it. He waves it off. When
>> it disappears, he sings:)

>> (SONG: "I DON'T REMEMBER YOU")

JACQUES (singing)
    I DON'T REMEMBER YOU,
    I DON'T REMEMBER YOU,
    I DON'T RECALL A SINGLE THING WE USED
      TO . . .
        (His song is broken off by another picture
        on the screen: the girl in various poses
        during the course of a day at a picnic, as
        described later in Laurie's speech in her
        first scene with JACQUES. Again he waves
        her away and speaks:)
No! I do not know who you are--and if I knew
you then--I have forgotten you now.
      (Now, more urgently, he sings:)
I DON'T REMEMBER YOU,
I DON'T REMEMBER YOU,
I DON'T RECALL A SINGLE THING WE USED
    TO SAY OR DO.

WHAT DANCING IN THE PARK?
WHAT LAUGHTER IN THE DARK?
WHAT SMOLDERING FIREPLACE
THAT LIT YOUR FACE WITH EVERY SPARK?

AND IF I LEFT YOU ONCE BEFORE
SOMEHOW I CAN'T RECALL IT ANY
    MORE.

THAT WAS ANOTHER GIRL,
YOU'RE NOT AT ALL LIKE HER,
THOUGH FOR AN INSTANT, WHEN I SAW YOU
I BELIEVED YOU WERE.

BUT I WAS WRONG!
THIS MOMENT IS NEW!

BECAUSE I CAN'T, I WON'T
I DON'T REMEMBER YOU.

(Even before the song finishes,
in the distance we hear the BOYS'
GLEE CLUB CHORUS, singing
"ST. PIERRE." The two songs
become counterpointed, then we
are in Laurie's classroom where
she is conducting the Glee Club
in "ST. PIERRE.")

(On screen, the faces of the BOYS' GLEE CLUB
appear one by one. The boys then appear on
stage, matching the photograph.)

JACQUES (ending "I DON'T REMEMBER YOU.")
BECAUSE I CAN'T, I WON'T.
I DON'T REMEMBER YOU.

(SONG: "ST. PIERRE")

LAURIE
AU-DESSUS DES COLLINES DE ST. PIERRE

BOYS
AU-DESSUS DES COLLINES DE ST. PIERRE

JACQUES
I DON'T REMEMBER YOU.

LAURIE
IL Y A SI BEAUCOUP DE FLEURS

BOYS
IL Y A SI BEAUCOUP DE FLEURS

LAURIE
QU'ILS FONT UN PARFUM DANS L'AIR

BOYS
QU'ILS FONT UN PARFUM DANS L'AIR

43

LAURIE (spoken)
  Parfum dans l'air

BOYS
  PARFUM DANS L'AIR

JACQUES
  I DON'T RECALL A SINGLE THING WE USED
    TO SAY OR DO

BOYS
  AU-DESSUS DES COLLINES DE ST. PIERRE

LAURIE
  LES VENTS SOUFFLENT TOUTES LES NUAGES

BOYS
  LES VENTS SOUFFLENT TOUTES LES NUAGES

LAURIE
  FAISANT CHAQUE JOUR UN JOUR CLAIR

BOYS
  FAISANT CHAQUE JOUR UN JOUR CLAIR

LAURIE
  JOUR UN JOUR CLAIR

JACQUES
  JOUR UN JOUR CLAIR

  ST. PIERRE!
  ST. PIERRE!
  MA MAISON,
  MON VILLAGE,
  MON PAYS,
  JE REVOIS!

BOYS
  ST. PIERRE!
  ST. PIERRE!
  MA MAISON,
  MON VILLAGE,
  MON PAYS,
  JE REVOIS!

44

JACQUES (gradually adding BOYS)
 AU-DESSUS DES COLLINES DE ST. PIERRE
 IL Y A SI BEAUCOUP DE FLEURS
 QU'ILS FONT UN PARFUM DANS L'AIR.

 AU-DESSUS DES COLLINES DE ST. PIERRE,
 LES VENTS SOUFFLENT TOUTES LES NUAGES
 FAISANT CHAQUE JOUR UN JOUR CLAIR.

BOYS
 ST. PIERRE!
 ST. PIERRE!
 MA MAISON
 MON VILLAGE,
 MON PAYS,
 JE REVOIS!

BOYS
 ST. PIERRE!

JACQUES
 ST. PIERRE!

BOYS
 ST. PIERRE!

JACQUES
 ST. PIERRE!

BOYS
 ST. PIERRE!

  (LAURIE MANNON concludes the conducting
  of the boys' choir in the song "ST. PIERRE."
  She turns and we see her now; a lovely young
  woman in her mid-twenties, fresh in outlook,
  direct in manner, sharp of wit. As she talks
  to the boys in the choir, JACQUES, who has
  been singing with the choir, unbeknownst to

them, now watches but does not join the
group. LAURIE talks to the boys.)

LAURIE
Well, that's very good! Fine! But I do think it
would be better if everybody would sing. Don't
you think so, Bibi?

BIBI (embarrassed)
Yes, mamselle.

LAURIE
Then why didn't you?
(From RODOLPHE, a titter.)
Is it a funny question, Rodolphe?
(From GANACHE, ANDRE and FRANCOIS,
more laughter.)
What is so funny? Bibi--why didn't you sing?

FOUFIE (lisping)
Because they won't let him sing!

BIBI
Be quiet, Foufie!

LAURIE
Who won't let him sing?

FOUFIE (pointing the boys out)
Rodolphe and Ganache!

LAURIE (to the boys)
Why? Ganache--Rodolphe--why?

FOUFIE
Because his voice is changing!

LAURIE
Quiet, Foufie! Ganache--I'm talking to you! Why?

46

GANACHE (laughing)

    Well, he sounds terrible, mamselle! Sometimes
he is a boy soprano and sometimes he is a girl
tenor!

THE BOYS (howling with laughter)

    Girl tenor! Boy soprano! Eh, Mamselle Bibi!
Sing, Mamselle!

        (The laughter grows. Now,
        luckily, the school bell.)

LAURIE

    Enough! No, Ganache, listen to me! Rodolphe,
you, too!

        (The group is out--except for BIBI,
        FOUFIE and GASTON. BIBI is hav-
        ing a hard time shaking his embar-
        rassment.)

Ganache, come back here! etc.

FOUFIE

    Don't be embarrassed because your voice is
changing! . . . sing, Bibi, sing!

LAURIE

    Out, Foufie. Gaston--out! You, too, Bibi.

        (FOUFIE and GASTON go. But BIBI
        slinks down. LAURIE tries to hide her
        commiseration by being gruff.)

I said, out! Schoolyard! With the others!

BIBI

    No! After this about the boy soprano, it is
going to be like hell out there!

LAURIE

    Take care--The language!

BIBI
    I think I am old enough to say "hell."

LAURIE (hiding the smile)
    What makes you old enough? One late night?

BIBI
    No, if I go out there I'll get in another fight with
    Ganache.

LAURIE
    I said, Out!

BIBI
    I'm sorry I do not have an apple for the teacher--
    how is a hard-boiled egg?
        (BIBI leaves the egg and hurries away.
        She looks at it ruminatively, with a
        fleeting smile. Now JACQUES makes
        his presence known. But he is puzzled
        by Laurie's looks: In the five years
        since he has seen her she has become
        a radiantly beautiful woman.)

JACQUES
    I am not sure, but I think . . . Laurie Mannon,
    yes?

LAURIE
    Yes. *Bonjour*, Monsieur Jacques.

JACQUES
    What is this "Monsieur"? I am plain Jacques.

LAURIE
    I would never call you a "plain Jacques."
    Anyway, "Monsieur" is what I called you five
    years ago . . . when you broke my bicycle.

JACQUES (surprised--and amused)
>   I broke your bicycle?

LAURIE
>   It was the day of the summer picnic. You borrowed
>   it to cross the bridge and when you came back, you
>   had the pedal in your hand.

JACQUES
>   Oh, but I fixed it, surely!

LAURIE (with a smile)
>   You've forgotten everything, haven't you? You
>   promised to fix it the following morning. The
>   following morning you were gone.

JACQUES
>   Oh, I am sorry to hear this!
>>   (Studying her, head to foot.)
>   And, I would like to make it up. You have be-
>   come a very beautiful woman and I would like to
>   fix your bicycle.

LAURIE
>   Don't make a donkey of yourself, Monsieur
>   Jacques. I did not send you a note about a
>   bicycle.

JACQUES (formally)
>   Ah, yes, your note, mamselle. Shall we discuss
>   it?

LAURIE (unexpectedly off-balance)
>   It's about--uh--about--
>>   (Holding up the egg.)
>   Bibi. He gave me this.

JACQUES
    I hope so.

LAURIE (in a flash of temper)
    Monsieur Jacques! You kept Bibi out until three
    o'clock last night! He fell asleep in class this
    morning!

JACQUES
    Ah, poor boy! I hope you did not wake him up!

LAURIE
    No! I covered him with a blanket and kept the
    class very quiet!

JACQUES
    Good--excellent!

LAURIE (quickly)
    Jacques, please, let him alone! You'll get him
    in trouble!

JACQUES
    Come now, you sound like my father! "Don't
    ruin him! Don't get him in trouble!" Trouble?
    You should have seen him last night! He was
    laughing so hard! That was a very happy boy!

LAURIE
    You think laughing is a sure sign of being happy?

JACQUES
    What sign is better--crying? Let me take your
    picture! Be happy!--cry for me!

LAURIE
    I have already done that!
            (Silence. This stops him. He is
            puzzled--and suddenly grave.)

JACQUES
     You . . . have cried for me?

LAURIE (quickly)
     Why did you come home, Jacques?

JACQUES
     What? I need a reason? My family--St. Pierre!
     . . .

LAURIE
     Oh, come now! You hate St. Pierre!

JACQUES (with a smile)
     You have found me out! . . . And you--an attrac-
     tive young girl like yourself--you do not hate it?

LAURIE
     No, I do not!

JACQUES
     What the devil do you like about it? What adven-
     ture happened in the bakery this morning? Did
     the postman make the same old joke about open-
     ing your love letters? Who was fascinating in
     church on Sunday? Nobody, except God! And I
     hear God, Himself, is getting so bored with St.
     Pierre that he hardly ever comes to church!

LAURIE
     What sweet memories you have of your home
     town. How long will you stay?

JACQUES
     Until my job is finished.

LAURIE
     What job?

JACQUES

I am always thinking of my work! Actually, I am here on a vacation.

LAURIE

Is that why you took a picture of the city hall this morning? And old Madame Dufour? And the postman?

JACQUES

A photographer takes pictures--he cannot help it!

LAURIE

Oh, really now! You are a professional photographer! You're going to sell these pictures and make money!

JACQUES

Is there anything wrong with that?

LAURIE

Don't you care about us at all?

JACQUES (laughing in exasperation)

Of course I do! I tell you, money has a bad name! No matter what you do for money--no matter how innocent--you are a scoundrel. Last night I took a picture of my father. He was upside down--teaching an acrobat how to stand on her head. If I show you that picture, you will laugh! But--if I sell it in a magazine and get paid for it--I am a monster! I sold my father! It's like love--you can be as promiscuous as you like--as long as you give it away free!

LAURIE

You don't see the difference?

JACQUES

What difference? Why take life so seriously? Is it so terrible?

52

LAURIE
    Is it a joke?

JACQUES
    For the most part, yes!
        (Quickly.)
    Let me show you! Spend the evening with me!

LAURIE
    No . . . I think not.

JACQUES (quieter now)
    I want you to go . . . please.

LAURIE
    No!

JACQUES
    Why not?

LAURIE
    Because, Monsieur Jacques, I think you are a
    liar!

JACQUES
    A liar! I lie to whom?

LAURIE
    Yourself mostly.
        (Then, with a wry smile.)
    And you even told me a little lie once.

JACQUES
    I did? . . . How? . . . What?

LAURIE
    There was a picnic, if you recall--and you
    singled me out for some reason, pigtails and all.
    You took me to the pines above the river--and

you sat beside me at night when they lit the
fire . . .
> (Then, with a laugh.)
. . . and you broke my bicycle. And you
promised to come around in the morning to
fix it, and . . .

(MUSIC)

LAURIE
> . . . and to kiss me. But in the morning you
> were gone without even a good-by.

JACQUES
> I'm sorry. I didn't remember anything.

LAURIE
> Then I must try not to remember, too.

(SONG: "I DON'T REMEMBER YOU" /REPRISE/)

LAURIE (singing)
> WHAT PICNIC BY THE MILL?
> WHAT RACE ACROSS THE HILL?
> WHAT FACE THAT SMILED "HELLO"
> ONE DAY BELOW MY WINDOWSILL?
>
> AND IF YOU HURT ME ONCE BEFORE
> SOMEHOW I CAN'T RECALL IT ANY MORE

JACQUES
> THAT WAS ANOTHER TIME,
> ANOTHER TIME AND PLACE

LAURIE
> ALTHOUGH YOU BEAR A FAINT RESEMBLANCE
> YOU'RE ANOTHER FACE.

54

LAURIE and JACQUES
    YES, WE WERE WRONG,
    THIS MOMENT IS NEW

JACQUES
    BECAUSE I CAN'T

LAURIE
    I WON'T

JACQUES and LAURIE
    I DON'T REMEMBER YOU!

(At conclusion of song, JACQUES starts to depart.
    As music reaches a crescendo, he returns,
    takes LAURIE in his arms, kisses her. Stage
    goes to darkness. And suddenly on the screen!
    A quick succession of projected photographs--
    full screen and split screen--of the boys in a
    violent fight. The last shot is an explosive
    moment of all the boys, BIBI in the midst of it!
    We see the still long enough to identify BIBI in
    the fight--then the photo is gone and--bright
    stage! The BOYS are all there matching the
    final photography.)

BIBI
    Uncle Jacques!

GANACHE (suddenly seeing JACQUES)
    Eh, watch out! He has a camera!
        (The fight is over. The boys run.)

JACQUES
    Hold it!

BIBI (mortified and enraged)
    Bon dieu-- you have been taking pictures--
55

when Ganache was making a fool out of me?

JACQUES
    Another one--stand still!

BIBI
    Stop it! No!

JACQUES
    Very good--hold it!

BIBI
    You stop it!
        (He grabs the camera.)

JACQUES
    Stop! I'll give you this picture two years from
    now, you will look at yourself and laugh! I'll
    cut a title on it: "Growing up!" And some day,
    you will look at that picture and say--"Oh, how
    I love it!"

BIBI
    Love what?

JACQUES
    What you loved last night, what you will love to-
    morrow! The world!
        (A pause. BIBI is held by this. He
        gives back the camera. Then quietly:)

BIBI
    Uncle Jacques--when you leave St. Pierre--I
    know you wouldn't take me with you--I mean you
    couldn't; but while you're here----
        (He cannot bring himself to finish the sentence.)

JACQUES
    While I'm here--what?

BIBI
  Nothing--never mind!

JACQUES
  Speak, boy!

BIBI
  No--it could never happen!

JACQUES
  Bibi! While I am here--how would you like to
  take a holiday from school--and be my assistant?

BIBI (a paean of joy)
  Oh, no!. . . You mean it? Oh, I can't stand it!
  Uncle Jacques, that's what I was---- Uncle
  Jacques, you mean it, do you mean it?

JACQUES (with wry enjoyment)
  I gather from your manner that you are not en-
  tirely opposed to this idea.
        (He slings his camera off his shoulder
        and hands it back to BIBI.)

BIBI
  Oh, no--for me? But yours? . . . I--what--no!

JACQUES
  I have five others. Take it.

BIBI
  Oh, God, I have to tell them! Rodolphe--you
  hear? Eh, Ganache! Look at this! It's mine!
  Francois--Andre!
        (He is crazy with delight.)

        (The other boys start reassembling.)

GANACHE
    Now what? You want to fight some more?

BIBI
    No--I want to take your picture!

GANACHE
    O. K.

RODOLPHE
    What's the matter? No film in the camera?

BIBI
    Yes, there is--I am going to be a photographer.

THE BOYS (disbelieving and derisive)
    You, a photographer! Oh, yes--I believe that!. . .
    Oh, sure! . . . Tell us another one, come on!

BIBI
    No--it is true! I am going to be assistant--to
    my uncle! Hold it!

                    (MUSIC)

RODOLPHE
    I don't believe it.
            (BIBI snaps one picture--of GANACHE. On
            the screen appears a picture of GANACHE--
            ugly, out of frame, ridiculous! The boys be-
            lieve BIBI. They start to shout:)

THE BOYS
    Eh--take my picture! . . . Eh, Bibi, look at
    me! . . . Look--I stand on my head, take my
    picture! . . . Eh, Bibi--my picture--me! . . .
    Look at me! Take me! Take me!

        (On the screen: a sequence of bad pictures,
                        58

as taken by BIBI. Pictures out of focus,
out of frame, lightstruck, too dark, double
exposures, the whole catalog of bad picture
taking--comic and crazy, forming a photo-
montage covering the entire screen. BIBI
starts to sing. His schoolmates join him in
song.)

        (SONG: "WITHOUT ME")

(As the song begins, the pictures fade,
leaving only their outline as a Mondrian-
like backing for the number.)

BIBI
    WITHOUT ME,
    WITHOUT ME,
    HOW COULD HE CONSIDER GOING ANYWHERE?
    LOOKING FOR HIS RIGHT ARM HE'D FIND
    IT WASN'T THERE,
    WITHOUT ME!

GANACHE
    WITHOUT ME!

BIBI
    WITHOUT ME!

GANACHE and CLAUDE
    WITHOUT ME!

BIBI
    WITHOUT ME!

GANACHE, CLAUDE and JULES
    WITHOUT ME!

BIBI
    WITHOUT ME!

59

GANACHE, CLAUDE and JULES
    WITHOUT ME!

BIBI, GANACHE, CLAUDE and JULES
    YOU WOULD HEAR HIM RAVING LIKE A
        LUNATIC,
    BEING A CAMERA WHOSE SHUTTER COULDN'T
        CLICK

ALL
    WITHOUT ME!
    WITHOUT ME!

    MY DISCRETION WILL KEEP HIM
    AT THE TOP OF HIS PROFESSION.
    IF I LEFT HIM
    I FEAR WITHOUT A DOUBT
    HE'D SOON BE DOWN AND OUT.

BIBI
    WITHOUT ME,
    WITHOUT ME,
    THOUGH IT'S QUITE A WEIGHT MY SHOULDERS
        HAVE TO BEAR,
    HOW COULD I ROB HIM OF MY CERTAIN SAVOIR
        FAIRE,
    KNOWING HE WOULDN'T KNOW TO GO FROM A
        TO B

ALL
    WITHOUT ME!
    WITHOUT ME!
    WITHOUT ME!
    WITHOUT ME!
    WITHOUT ME!

60

BIBI
>THOUGH YOU THINK OF ME AS

ALL
>SUPERFLUOUS

BIBI
>HE THINKS OF ME AS

ALL
>SUPERLATIVE.

BIBI
>THOUGH YOU THINK OF ME AS

ALL
>RIDICULOUS

BIBI
>HE THINKS OF ME AS REMARKABLE

ALL
>SOMETHING VERY SPECIAL
>SOMETHING VERY RARE,
>SOMETHING MAGNIFIQUE,
>TRES EXTRAORDINAIRE!
>
>WITHOUT ME!
>WITHOUT ME!
>COULD HE HOPE TO WIN ANOTHER LOVING
> CUP?
>KNOWING HE CAN'T BEGIN TO KNOW WHICH
> END IS UP
>WITHOUT ME!
>WITHOUT ME!
>WITHOUT ME!
>
>HIS EXISTENCE
>DEPENDS ON MY INVALUABLE ASSISTANCE.

IF I LEFT HIM
I FEEL WITHIN MY HEART
THE FEAR HE'D FALL APART.
I FEEL WITHOUT A DOUBT
HE'D SOON BE DOWN AND OUT.

(DANCE INTERLUDE)

ALL
WITHOUT ME!
WITHOUT ME!
COULD HE HOPE TO WIN ANOTHER LOVING
CUP?
KNOWING HE CAN'T BEGIN TO KNOW WHICH
END IS UP
WITHOUT ME!
WITHOUT ME!
WITHOUT ME!
WITHOUT ME!
WITHOUT ME!
(At conclusion, the boys are sprawled
all over the stage. BIBI, atop the
Jungle Jim, photographs them, and the
pictures appear on the screen.)

(As the boys leave, we see SUZANNE
threading her way through them, and
we are now back in the Bonnard garden.)

SUZANNE (offstage)
Breakfast! Breakfast everyone!

(SUZANNE enters.)

SUZANNE
Breakfast, everybody! A lovely morning--
breakfast in the garden! Papa! Louis--Felice--
chez nous! Breakfast! (She goes out again,

calling the family to breakfast.)

(LOUIS and FELICE enter, accompanied by their
three daughters, NANETTE, GILLIE and
ANNABELLE.)

LOUIS
You are certain we are invited for breakfast?

FELICE
Why do you ask? Are you deaf?--you did not
hear her?--or are you already drunk so early
in the morning?

LOUIS
You are speaking to me?

FELICE
You--you drink like a hole in the ground. You
are something one should not throw to the dogs!

LOUIS
Do not be so holy! The king is not your cousin!

FELICE
Quiet! You lose so many chances to be quiet!

LOUIS
Take care, Felice--the mustard is rising in my
nose!

FELICE
How long has it been since I called you a drunkard?

LOUIS
Five minutes.

(GRANDPERE enters.)

GRANDPERE

    The proper name for him is thief! What did you
do with my pictures?

LOUIS

    He calls me a thief; it's to make one cry.

GRANDPERE

    If I slap a mosquito you cry.

LOUIS

    Who took your pictures?

GRANDPERE

    You! Twenty-three pictures--including two
Madame du Barrys and one Marie Antoinette
eating cake in the bathtub! . . .

LOUIS

    You call me more names and I will inform your
girl friend the Widow La Touche you are courting
her for her money!
      (He sits down.)

GRANDPERE

    Of course I court her for her money! What else
does she have?--youth?--beauty?--teeth? . . .
What did you find out about last night?

LOUIS

    Nothing! You found out something?

      (SUZANNE reenters R.)

GRANDPERE

    Nothing. Sh--be quiet!

SUZANNE

    What is the shush? What is the "be quiet"?

GRANDPERE
>Never mind.
>>(To LOUIS.)
>They <u>were</u> together--you know that.

LOUIS
>I know. I saw him with Laurie at the cafe at
>one o'clock in the morning.

>>(PHILLIPPE enters.)

GRANDPERE
>And then? . . . Well?

LOUIS
>How the devil do I know? Should I go to her and
>say: "Mamselle Laurie--my father, who has a
>long nose, wants to know if you made love to my
>brother Jacques last night!" Shall I do that?

GRANDPERE
>N-no. It would not be good.
>>(By now the rest of the family are
>>deeply involved. They say, weightily:)

PHILIPPE
>Very embarrassing . . .

SUZANNE
>Dreadful! . . .

FELICE
>Not good--no!

GRANDPERE
>But you could say it in a different way. You
>could be a poet. "Mamselle Laurie--last
>evening did a bluebird fly across the moon?
>Was there a year of springtime in one night?"

LOUIS (standing up, by FELICE)
How did you say it about the bluebird?

GRANDPERE
Did a bluebird fly across the moon?

LOUIS
Felice, stand still--I want to practice it.
(To FELICE.)
Did a bluebird fly across the----

FELICE
You give me a bluebird, I'll give you such a
smack!

LOUIS
It will not work, Papa. She is not Laurie, and I
am not a poet.

GRANDPERE
Never mind. When we see Laurie, I have another
way to find out.

SUZANNE
Just a moment! I have invited her to breakfast--
and you will not embarrass her! No prying looks
and no questions!

GRANDPERE
Who needs questions? The minute they are together we will know if the bluebird flew across
the moon!

LOUIS
Absolutely! They will make eyes at each other,
they will throw kisses!

GRANDPERE
Ox!

LOUIS
  What!

GRANDPERE
  I said you are an ox! If a bluebird flew across
  the moon last night, this morning they will not
  make eyes at each other, and they will not throw
  kisses! No! They will pretend to be strangers!
  He will call her "Mamselle" and she will call
  him "Monsieur"! They will be so polite--like
  a tinkle of tiny little teacups!

PHILIPPE
  I think he is right.

FELICE
  Sh--quiet--here he comes.

ALL
  Good morning . . . Good morning, Jacques . . .
  Good morning, everyone!

LOUIS
  . . . I don't think a bluebird flew across the
  moon.

GRANDPERE
  Ox! How can you tell until you see the other one?

JACQUES
  Bluebird? What bluebird? What is going on?

LOUIS
  I tell you, I know! No bluebird flew across the
  moon! If a bluebird flew, I will walk naked from
  here to the post office.

PHILIPPE and SUZANNE
  Sh--sh! Look--look! . . . It's Laurie--it's Laurie!

(LAURIE enters.   There are general
    greetings.)

ALL
    Bonjour, Laurie . . . Welcome, Laurie . . .
    How pretty you look this morning!
        (Silence. The moment of truth. The
        only people who have not greeted each
        other are JACQUES and LAURIE. Then:)

JACQUES (with a slight, formal bow)
    Bonjour, mamselle.

LAURIE (with a slow, formal nod)
    Bonjour, Monsieur Jacques.
        (Absolute silence. The family look at
        one another, trying to hide their smiles.
        Now, slowly, deliberately, GRANDPERE
        crosses the stage to LOUIS. As LOUIS
        docilely turns his back to his father,
        GRANDPERE helps LOUIS off with his
        coat--he's going to walk to the post office.
        As LOUIS turns and GRANDPERE starts
        to unbutton Louis' shirt, the family bursts
        into laughter.)

JACQUES
    What is it? What is going on?

SUZANNE
    Never mind! Breakfast!--breakfast, everyone!

FELICE (overlapping, to LOUIS)
    Put your clothes on and come to breakfast.
    Philippe! Bibi, Bibi! Gillie, come and eat!

68

(GILLIE enters, then BIBI. BIBI has a note in his
   hand.)

BIBI
   Good morning! Good morning, everyone! Papa,
   would you sign this? Mamselle Mannon cannot
   give her permission unless you sign it! Please
   hurry--she has to go to school!

PHILIPPE
   She has to go to school? How about you?
      (Waving paper.)

BIBI
   Please sign it! Hurry!

PHILIPPE
   You do not make an objection if I read it, *non?*

SUZANNE
   Laurie, what is in the letter? Read it, Philippe!

PHILIPPE (reading)
   "Dear Mamselle Mannon. Please excuse my son
   from all classes for three days since he is absolutely indispensable----"
      (He stops. To BIBI.)
   Indispensable is with an "i."

BIBI
   No. With an "a," Papa.

SUZANNE
   Name of heaven, Bibi is indispensable? To whom?
   For what?

JACQUES
   Me! My assistant!

69

PHILIPPE
 Why? You are here on a job?

JACQUES
 I'm always on a job!

PHILIPPE
 Here in St. Pierre?

JACQUES
 Why not? St. Pierre has no flowers, no birds?
 Has the world ever seen the roses of St. Pierre?
 I'll take pictures--he will be my assistant!

PHILIPPE
 For this he has to be taken out of school?

JACQUES
 Ah, for only three days, Philippe. Come now,
 this is not serious, *non?* He tells me he is at the
 head of the class--he will catch up!
  (To LAURIE.)
 This is true, Laurie?

LAURIE
 Oui.

JACQUES (as she nods, he sails ahead)
 Bon! Bibi--hurry with your breakfast!

PHILIPPE (stopping JACQUES)
 Jacques! One minute!
  (To LAURIE.)
 Laurie, you approve of this?

LAURIE
 Whether I approve or not, there are certain rules!
 I cannot say yes without a responsible signature!

JACQUES (gently)
   Sign it, Philippe!

SUZANNE
   Yes, do sign it, my dear.

PHILLIPE (looking at his watch; to BIBI)
   It is late. Go to school.
            (Gently, almost affectionately, JACQUES
            takes the watch out of Philippe's hand.
            The watch is attached to a heavy chain,
            to Philippe's vest. JACQUES, ribbing
            PHILIPPE good naturedly, hands his
            brother a pen.)

JACQUES
   Here--I will hold your heavy watch while you
   hold the pen. Sign it.

PHILIPPE (annoyed; snatching back his watch)
   I will hold my own watch, thank you! If you think
   you can make a joke out of this----

JACQUES
   Why not? What is so terrible? You are worried
   that the boy will miss something in school? I
   will make it up to him! He will see things he
   has never seen before! He will do things he has
   never done!

PHILIPPE
   I have no doubt of that!
            (An instant. Now JACQUES changes
            tactics.)

JACQUES (pleadingly)
   Philippe--please! He will see things through a
   new lens! Is not bad to change the lens! It makes
   a new world!

71

PHILIPPE
    The answer is no!

BIBI
    Please, Papa!

JACQUES (simultaneously)
    Philippe, do not force him to go to school!

PHILIPPE (lashing back)
    Don't use the word "force"! I never force him
    to anything! The first night you arrived I told
    you--I never lay a hand on him! Never! And if
    you recall, you invited him to the vaudeville and
    I did not say no, I let him decide! And he did
    not go, did he?
        (Silence. Now PHILIPPE speaks in a
        more mollifying tone, almost as if he
        pities JACQUES.)
    You see, Jacques--we have between us--Bibi
    and me--a certain respect. Father to son--
    and son to father. So if I ask Bibi to tear up
    the paper, he will do it. Out of respect. To
    me, to his mother . . . his school . . . his
    family.
        (He turns to BIBI. Gently.)
    Bibi . . . tear it up, if you please.

BIBI (a deeply painful moment, then:)
    . . . No!

PHILIPPE (hurt)
    Bibi . . . Son! . . . Please!

BIBI (grabbing the paper and holding it out to SUZANNE)
    No! *Maman*--please! You sign it!

PHILIPPE (sharply)
    Suzanne! No!

72

SUZANNE (an instant, then:)
I--I'm sorry, Bibi.

BIBI (help where? Turning to LAURIE)
Mamselle, you know I can make the work up!
You don't really need this paper!

LAURIE
Yes, I do, Bibi. Unless some member of your
family signs it----

BIBI (interrupting)
Member of my----
(On an outcry of inspiration, he
turns to JACQUES.)
Uncle Jacques!

PHILLIPE (as BIBI carries the paper to JACQUES)
No! Jacques--I beg you----

BIBI
Uncle Jacques--sign it! Please!

PHILIPPE
No, Jacques!

JACQUES
Philippe----

PHILIPPE
Stay out of this!

JACQUES
Like hell I will!

BIBI
Please, Uncle Jacques!

JACQUES (angry, wavering, looking from PHILIPPE
    to BIBI)
    Bibi, if I were your father . . . But I am not
    your father . . .

BIBI (interrupting, with an outcry)
    Oh, I wish you were!

SUZANNE
    Bibi!
        (The shock holds the stillness. Quietly,
        PHILIPPE turns away. JACQUES sees
        Philippe's deep hurt. Quickly--to mend
        the breech between father and son:)

JACQUES
    He did not mean it, Philippe!

BIBI (weeping now)
    Please--Uncle Jacques--sign it!

JACQUES (gently)
    I am sorry, Bibi!

PHILIPPE (turning back to BIBI)
    It is late. Go to school!

BIBI
    No!

PHILIPPE
    I said go to school!

BIBI
    Like hell I will!
PHILIPPE
    Those are your uncle's words!
        (He slaps BIBI across the face.)

74

SUZANNE
    Philippe! No!
        (BIBI rushes away.)
    Oh, Bibi!
        (A breath of silence, then, alone,
        away from the group, a soft sound
        of weeping. It's LOUIS, quite
        motionless, but crying forlornly.
        GRANDPERE crosses to him, and
        hardly looking at LOUIS, gives
        him his own immaculate handker-
        chief. NANETTE giggles. GRAND-
        PERE turns to her.)

GRANDPERE (softly)
    Stop that. A father is a simpleton, yes--but
    do not laugh at him.

FELICE (quietly)
    Come, simpleton.

GRANDPERE
    Don't you call him a simpleton!

FELICE
    You just called him that yourself!

GRANDPERE
    I am his father.

SUZANNE
    If anybody is a simpleton, it's my husband!
    Why did you slap that boy?

PHILIPPE (pointing to JACQUES)
    Don't blame it on me--blame it on that trouble-
    maker! It's Jacques' fault!

LOUIS
    You made the trouble for yourself!

PHILIPPE
I did no such thing!

SUZANNE
Yes, you did!

PHILIPPE
Was there any trouble
before Jacques came?
No! As soon as
Jacques arrived--
trouble, arguments,
fights!

GRANDPERE
You all love to
fight--Jacques or no
Jacques! This
family loves to fight!

SUZANNE
There is no sense
to this family! Why
did I marry into it
anyway?

FELICE
Jacques made the
trouble--only Jacques
made it!

GILLIE
He did not! He only tried
to do something for Bibi!

FELICE
Jacques always makes
trouble when he comes!

LOUIS
Jacques! Jacques!
Everybody always
blames everything on
Jacques!

FELICE
You always stand up
for Jacques--because
you are exactly like
Jacques!

(The family departs. Left onstage are
JACQUES and LAURIE. An instant.
She applauds him lightly, mockingly.
Then she leaves. JACQUES sings the
reprise of "THE HAPPY TIME.")

76

(SONG: "THE HAPPY TIME" /REPRISE/)

JACQUES (singing)
    REMEMBER MY JOURNEY HOME TO ST. PIERRE
    THE JOY I BROUGHT JUST BEING THERE

(MUSIC)

JACQUES
    REMEMBER EACH GENTLE VOICE
    EACH DELICATE SOUND
    REMEMBER THE WAVES OF LOVE
    IN WHICH I WAS VERY NEARLY DROWNED.

    REMEMBER THEY SPARKLED LIKE A CHRIST-
      MAS TREE
    AT JUST THE VERY SIGHT OF ME.
    FOR MY VISITS ALWAYS GUARANTEE
    THE HAPPY TIME.
      (JACQUES departs. Lights fade.)

CURTAIN

ACT TWO

AT RISE OF CURTAIN: The stage is dark except for
the glow of a single small red-orange light bulb.
It's a photographer's darkroom light. JACQUES
is developing pictures. From time to time during the scene, as he waits for the hypo to work,
he looks at some opened telegrams and at the con-
tents of a small fancy box. These objects give
him a moment of pleasure and poignancy. Even
before he speaks--and perhaps during his song,
too--the photographs he is developing seem to
float up on the screen as if shimmering out of the
hypo and wash waters.)

(During the song--shots of people and moments we've
already seen--and, perhaps, of moments we are
yet to see.)

(SONG: "AMONG MY YESTERDAYS")

JACQUES (singing)
WAS IT REALLY ALL THAT SWEET
IN THAT HOUSE AND ALONG THAT STREET?
MEMORY CLOUDS IN A THOUSAND WAYS,
WALKING AMONG MY YESTERDAYS.

DID IT HAPPEN? WAS IT REAL?
EYES CAN SEE WHAT THE HEART CAN
    FEEL
VISIONS VANISH BENEATH THE GAZE,
WALKING AMONG MY YESTERDAYS.

78

HOLD! HOLD! HOLD!
WAIT FOR ME!
LIGHT THE PICTURE, LET ME SEE!

NOW AND THEN THE IMAGE CLEARS.
TRUTH IS PLAIN, THEN IT DISAPPEARS,
ONE MORE TRICK THAT THE CAMERA PLAYS,
WALKING AMONG MY YESTERDAYS.

HOLD! HOLD! HOLD!
WAIT FOR ME!
LIGHT THE PICTURE, LET ME SEE!

SOUVENIRS OF THE PAST REMAIN,
BITS OF PLEASURE AND SCRAPS OF PAIN,
LOVE MAY PASS BUT THE PERFUME STAYS,
WALKING AMONG MY YESTERDAYS.

HOLD! HOLD! HOLD!
YESTERDAYS . . .

(As the song concludes, FOUFIE returns, crossing.
    JACQUES calls to him.)

JACQUES
        Foufie, have you seen Bibi?
            (FOUFIE shrugs.)

(At the same instant, a group of boys rush on from
    the opposite side of the stage with more pictures.
    JACQUES vainly attempts to find BIBI in the
    confusion.)

JACQUES
        Where is Bibi? Have you seen my nephew?
            (As the boys scatter, JACQUES is
            left calling after them.)

Come back here!

(As he calls, BIBI appears. He is filthy dirty, his
clothes are awry, his hair needs combing. His
manner is as cocky, as self-certain as he hither-
to has been sensitive; a totally changed boy . . .
well, superficially changed. He walks with a
strut, twirling the Tyrolean hat around his index
finger. He whistles with easy arrogance--he
might be GANACHE!)

JACQUES (silence; then:)
Well! Where have you been all day?

BIBI (with superiority)
Who wants to know this?

JACQUES (angry)
You don't know me? My name is Uncle Jacques!

BIBI (lording it)
Enchanté, Monsieur.
(And he starts to pass JACQUES)

JACQUES (trying to stop him)
Bibi--wait! Why are you angry at <u>me</u>?

BIBI (whirling on him, an instant's flash of the true
hurt)
Why didn't you sign my note to Mademoiselle
Mannon?

JACQUES
A question is not answered with a question. What
did you do today?

BIBI
I did what I wanted to do!

JACQUES (with a wry smile)
What? You did something bad?

BIBI
If you do what you want to do, does it mean it
has to be bad?

JACQUES
In my experience, yes.

BIBI
Then you have a terrible experience!

JACQUES
Mm . . . yes.

(GRANDPERE enters.)

GRANDPERE
Ah, both together, of course! Where the devil
were you, both of you! You! Go home! Your
mother worries about you!
(BIBI starts off.)
That is not the way home.

BIBI
I know!
(BIBI exits.)

GRANDPERE (to JACQUES)
You see that? You see your influence on this
boy? And you, where have you been all day?

JACQUES
I took a room in the St. Pierre Hotel.

GRANDPERE
No! Even you would not do something so
foolish! Come home!

81

JACQUES
    Oh, no! This time you will not make peace in
    the family. I will stay in the hotel.
        (Starts off.)

GRANDPERE
    I hope you did not sit on the bed.

JACQUES
    What did you say?

GRANDPERE
    I said, I hope you did not sit on the bed.

JACQUES
    Why? The beds are hard?

GRANDPERE
    Ah, if that were the only thing the matter with
    the beds----
        (Pretending to be inconspicuous about
        it, he starts to scratch himself.)

JACQUES
    Why the devil do you scratch?

GRANDPERE
    It makes one to itch just to think about them?

JACQUES
    Them? Who?

GRANDPERE
    Not who--what! A bedbug is not a who!

JACQUES
    Bedbugs! No! You're a liar, Papa!
82

GRANDPERE
    Wait! Don't move! You did sit on the bed!
    Don't move!

JACQUES (turning reflexively)
    Where? What?

GRANDPERE
    Ah, you *stupide*, you moved!

JACQUES
    Where? There aren't any!

GRANDPERE
    Too late! You have to look fast if you want to
    see a bedbug!

JACQUES
    I don't want to see a bedbug!

GRANDPERE
    You don't want to see anything!

JACQUES
    Papa, I have been thinking. What would happen if
    I stayed in St. Pierre?

GRANDPERE
    What kind of foolishness is this? Who wants
    you here?

JACQUES
    You do, Papa!

GRANDPERE
    I do not even like you!

JACQUES
    Yes, you do, Papa . . . you like me best of all.

GRANDPERE

Eh! Each one of my children thinks I like him
the best! Why not? . . . A good father is a good
liar!

JACQUES

You do like me the best . . . and you dislike me
the most.

GRANDPERE

What the devil does that mean?

JACQUES

Papa, what do I have to do to get a little pat on
the head? "Boy, you did that very well." What
do I have to do?

GRANDPERE

When you lie to me, shall I say you did that very
well?

JACQUES

When? When did I lie to you?

GRANDPERE

The first day you arrived. When you told me
you had come for a visit. That was not true,
Jacques. You came to take pictures of us and
all St. Pierre.

JACQUES

How did you find that out?

GRANDPERE

How? I accidentally went into your room and I
saw an envelope, and I accidentally opened it up,
and in it was a big contract, and I sat down and
read it--accidentally. Now I want you to stop

this foolishness, tear up that idiotic contract . . .
they are underpaying you anyhow . . . and come
back home!

JACQUES
And if I did, do you suppose Philippe would welcome me with open arms?

(LAURIE enters)

GRANDPERE
Open arms or not, you will have to come tonight.
(He sees LAURIE.) Ah! Laurie--I am glad to see
you. I was about to tell Jacques why you all have
to come home with me, at least for tonight. You
tell him.

LAURIE
Me? But I do not know.

GRANDPERE
Name of a blue cow! You do not want to miss it,
do you?

JACQUES
Miss . . . what?

GRANDPERE
My party

JACQUES
Party? . . . What party?

GRANDPERE
My birthday! I am giving myself a surprise
party--a surprise birthday party!

JACQUES
    It is not your birthday!

GRANDPERE
    That is what is so surprising about it!

JACQUES
    Every time anything unpleasant happens in the
    family, suddenly a birthday party! We have
    celebrated five hundred times, Papa.

GRANDPERE
    But of course! I have decided to stay alive until
    you get smart! Which means I am going to live
    forever! Now--a big party--what is the biggest
    place in town? The gymnasium! Jacques, you'll
    be there!

JACQUES
    No, Papa, I will not go.

LAURIE
    I'm not angry at anybody! I'll go--and I'll drag
    him along with me!

GRANDPERE
    Eh! For this girl a man might not be such a fool
    if he decided to stay home! Don't move!
        (He picks an imaginary bedbug off
        Jacques' shoulder, drops it on the
        floor and stamps on it)
    I will expect you there.
        (GRANDPERE departs quickly.
        LAURIE is alerted.)

LAURIE
    What did that mean--"stay home"?

JACQUES
    I told him I might consider staying in St. Pierre.

LAURIE
     You mean you led him on to believe you might
     stay?

JACQUES (defensive)
     I didn't "lead him on"! I meant it!

LAURIE
     And now me!

JACQUES
     No! I'm not leading you on! I mean it!
          (An instant; LAURIE is deeply touched.)

LAURIE
     That may be the nicest offer you've ever made.
          (Gently.)
     But nobody will ever accept it!

JACQUES (quickly)
     You mean you don't <u>want</u> me to stay!

LAURIE
     Stop it! I'd give my eye teeth to have you stay!

JACQUES (breaking out--the injured, unwanted male)
     You have a hell of a way of showing it! So does
     my father! Everybody loves me and wants me to
     take the next train out of town!

(MUSIC)

(Jacques' outburst, rather than disturbing LAURIE,
     makes her happy. She smiles at him--in an al-
     most motherly way.)

LAURIE (gently)
     But I do love you, Jacques.

JACQUES (snapping)
   "I love you--here's your hat!"

LAURIE (very quietly)
   I love you . . . please stay.

JACQUES
   You don't love me as much as a little fat hotel
   manager in Budapest! Every time I leave the
   hotel, he cries! And in London there is an old
   chambermaid--seventy-five years old----

      (SONG: "PLEASE STAY"[REPRISE])

LAURIE (singing)
   I READ A BOOK ON LONDON,
   IT'S BEAUTIFUL, I KNOW----

JACQUES
   When I arrive she puts a note on my pillow:
   "Welcome home to room three-o-six!"

LAURIE
   SUCH FUN TO BE IN LONDON: DON'T GO!

JACQUES
   And in Lisbon last year----

LAURIE
   AND LISBON MUST BE PRETTY
   AROUND THIS TIME OF YEAR----

JACQUES
   --there is a family of wine-growers----

LAURIE
   JUST MARVELOUS IN LISBON: STAY HERE.

JACQUES
    And Venice--Laurie--Venice!

LAURIE
    AND VENICE TAKES YOUR BREATH AWAY,
    THEY SAY.
    STAY!
        (She stops singing. They are very
        close. She speaks softly:)
    Please stay.
        (Absolute silence. Then:)

JACQUES
    I'm staying, Laurie.

(He puts his arm around her; they walk off together;
    as GRANDPERE, near the top of a red self-sup-
    porting ladder, is pushed onstage and any props
    indicating the street scene are pulled up or off.
    The BOYS' glee club and THE SIX ANGELS are
    helping. GRANDPERE is directing the decorat-
    ing of the gymnasium with crepe paper streamers
    from a central overhead /and quickly removable/
    location to various convenient places around the
    stage, where they are very loosely attached.)

GRANDPERE
    . . . and furthermore, we don't have much time
    --we must get this party ready as quickly as pos-
    sible! You down there--and you and you--you will
    be in charge of the balloons! You boys over there--
    you take care of the streamers and the noisemakers!
    And the rest of you get the paper hats ready! . . .
    Now, where is Foufie?

FOUFIE
    Here I am!

GRANDPERE
    Did you go and talk to my family?

FOUFIE
    Yes, I did.

GRANDPERE
    Did you tell them we are having a party here?

FOUFIE
    Yes, I did.

GRANDPERE
    Did you tell them that they are invited to stay
    home?

FOUFIE
    Yes, I did.

GRANDPERE
    Good! That means they will be here shortly! We
    must prepare! Foufie--you say you can play the
    piano?

FOUFIE
    Yes, I can!

GRANDPERE
    Then play something! . . . with a little boom
    boom boom boom!
        (FOUFIE plays boom boom boom boom on a
        spinet piano UR or on the orchestra piano
        with a spot on him.)
    Do it again!
        (FOUFIE plays boom boom boom boom,
        somewhat differently.)

GRANDPERE
    Good! Now we have everything we need! But,
    most of all, we have . . . me!

    (SONG: "THE LIFE OF THE PARTY")

GRANDPERE (singing)
    OF COURSE IT'S FUN TO WEAR A RED PAPER
    HAT,

90

OF COURSE IT'S GOOD TO KNOW THE WINE
  ISN'T FLAT,
BUT THOUGH YOU TAKE A CERTAIN COM-
  FORT FROM THAT
YOU BETTER HAVE ME THERE,
THE LIFE OF THE PARTY!

OF COURSE IT'S NICE TO SEE THE STREAMERS
  ARE FLUNG,
TO KNOW THE GUEST LIST IS APPEALINGLY
  YOUNG,
BUT IF YOU WANT TO HEAR THAT BELL
  REALLY RUNG
YOU BETTER HAVE ME THERE,
THE LIFE OF THE PARTY!

OH, NO!
YOU WOULDN'T WANT THE NIGHT TO BE A
  BORE.
TO HAVE THEM GAZING FONDLY AT THE DOOR,
SO WHY NOT HAVE THE GUARANTEE
THE FUN'S ABOUT TO BEGIN
WHEN I COME SAUNTERING IN.

OF COURSE IT'S NICE WHEN CANDLES GLEAM
  EVERYWHERE,
WHEN THERE ARE LANTERNS SWINGING HIGH
  IN THE AIR,
BUT IF YOU REALLY WANT A SNAPPY AFFAIR
  YOU BETTER HAVE ME THERE,
THE LIFE OF THE PARTY
TO BRING THE PARTY TO LIFE!

GRANDPERE and BOYS
    BOOM BOOM BOOM BOOM
    BOOM BOOM BOOM BOOM
    BOOM BOOM BOOM BOOM BOOM BOOM
      BOOM BOOM BOOM BOOM BOOM BOOM

BOYS
    BOOM BOOM BOOM BOOM
    BOOM BOOM BOOM BOOM

BOOM BOOM BOOM BOOM BOOM BOOM
  BOOM BOOM BOOM BOOM BOOM BOOM
BOOM BOOM BOOM BOOM
BOOM BOOM BOOM BOOM
BOOM BOOM BOOM BOOM
BOOM BOOM BOOM AHHHH! . . .

GRANDPERE
    IF YOUR FESTIVITIES INCLUDE A SOIREE
    YOU OUGHT TO GIVE IT EASE THE EASIEST
      WAY
    BESIDE THE CAVIAR AND CHOCOLATE
      SOUFFLE
    YOU BETTER HAVE ME THERE,
    THE LIFE OF THE PARTY!

    OF COURSE IT'S NICE TO SEE A YELLOW
      BALLOON,
    TO HEAR THE ORCHESTRA IS PLAYING IN
      TUNE,
    BUT IF YOU REALLY LIKE IT HIGH AS THE
      MOON
    YOU BETTER HAVE ME THERE,
    THE LIFE OF THE PARTY!

    OH, NO!
    YOU WOULDN'T WANT IT GETTING VERY DULL,
    BECOMING ONE UNINTERRUPTED LULL,
    SO WHY NOT HAVE THE GUARANTEE
    THE FUN'S ABOUT TO BEGIN
    WHEN I COME SWAGGERING IN.
        (GRANDPERE comes down from the
        ladder doing a little swaggering "kick
        step" as he descends.)

          ORCHESTRA
  (OF COURSE IT'S NICE TO GIVE THEM
    COLORFUL LIGHTS)
  (OR LOVELY LADIES DRESSED IN LAVENDER
    TIGHTS)

(BUT IF YOU REALLY WANT THE NIGHT OF
ALL NIGHTS)

GRANDPERE   BOYS
YOU BETTER HAVE
ME THERE,
THE LIFE OF THE   THE LIFE OF THE
PARTY!   PARTY!

THE LIFE OF THE   THE LIFE OF THE
PARTY!   PARTY!

TO BRING THE PARTY TO LIFE

(At end of "THE LIFE OF THE PARTY"
JACQUES, LAURIE and BIBI arrive.)

JACQUES
Hold it!

GRANDPERE (to the BOYS)
See-he is here! He heard we were having a
good time--he got jealous!

JACQUES
A man is five hundred years old, I have to take
his picture. Hold it!

(The BONNARD FAMILY arrives. Proud, stiff,
alien; they carry black balloons. GRANDPERE
sees them; he is as stand-offish as they are.
He will not talk to them except through an
intermediary--LAURIE.)

GRANDPERE
Who invited these people? Who are they?

LOUIS (to LAURIE)
Tell the old goat we are his family!

PHILIPPE
His flesh and blood.

93

GRANDPERE
    Why are you here? You were not invited.

PHILIPPE
    We are here because it is your birthday.

GRANDPERE
    It is not my birthday! That is why I am having
    a party! I was born in the year of the Great
    Flood, nine days after the water went down. So,
    my birthday is the ninth!

PHILIPPE
    Exactly! And that is today!

GRANDPERE
    Today? Can he be right? Bibi, can he be right?

BIBI
    My father is never wrong on matters such as
    this.
        (PHILIPPE crosses to BIBI.)

PHILIPPE
    Thank you. I'm glad you helped to straighten
    this matter out. Thank you, my son.

GRANDPERE (ecstatic)
    Truly my birthday! Then let them stay! Boom
    boom boom boom!

(REPRISE "THE LIFE OF THE PARTY." Now
    they start to encore it, this time with a wilder,
    more driving rhythm. Suddenly, GRANDPERE
    clutches at his chest.)

EVERYBODY
    Grandpere!...Papa, what is it?...Papa?
94

PHILIPPE
    Bibi--hurry! Get the doctor!
        (BIBI rushes out.)

SUZANNE
    Get a chair! He must lie down!

GRANDPERE
    No--no--let me down!
        (Angry, crotchety.)
    What is this? Let me down! I say, let me down!
        (As they put him in a lounging
        chair.)
    A man lets out a belch and you lift him up like
    a roulade of beef!

JACQUES (the quickest to adopt the tone his father
        wishes)
    A silly old man is lucky to have somebody to
    pick him up!

GRANDPERE
    Shut up and get me something to drink!

PHILIPPE
    Until the doctor comes--water!

JACQUES
    Cognac!

LOUIS
    Wine, you fool!

GRANDPERE
    These are my sons! One says water, one says
    wine and one says cognac. What do you say,
    my dear?

SUZANNE
     All of them!
          (As PHILIPPE gives a disapproving
          look. Quickly:)
     In moderation!

GRANDPERE
     Moderation! What an unpleasant word!
          (Making a toast.)
     I drink wine--to my three miserable sons!
          (He starts to drink the wine. Before
          he has had more than a sip, PHILIPPE
          takes the glass away.)

PHILIPPE
     That's enough!

GRANDPERE
     What the devil? This is the first time I have had
     one of these attacks? I have had dozens of them!
     Take my temperature, take my pulse. Jacques,
     take my pulse--stronger than yours--take it!
          (Grabs glass and sips wine.)
     Well?

JACQUES
     Hmm. Nothing. Absolutely nothing! I think the
     old fool is dead.

LOUIS
     Are you dead?

JACQUES
     How long has he been dead?

GRANDPERE
     I will live to plant a daisy on your grave.

JACQUES
    My dear man, you are in bad condition. I will
    have to put you on a diet. Wet toast, warm milk,
    and, on the rare occasion, a mushed egg!

GRANDPERE
    Better to die!

JACQUES
    And no more wine and no more widow!

GRANDPERE
    Then I am dead!
        (He starts to get up.)

PHILIPPE
    Wait! Sit still! Where do you think you are
    going?

GRANDPERE
    Home--to die!

PHILIPPE
    No--wait! You cannot walk all the way home un-
    less Doctor Gagneau allows it.

GRANDPERE
    What--you think I will listen to him? Last Friday
    Doctor Gagneau told Felice she had an incurable
    disease. On Saturday she broke wind and was
    miraculously cured! . . . A lovely party . . .
    The loveliest. Good night.
        (As GRANDPERE raises his arm to
        wave to everybody:)

JACQUES
    Hold it!
        (JACQUES takes the picture and the
        instant freezes. *Click!* On the screen

97

a portrait picture of GRANDPERE--not
as he is now, but thirty years younger,
as snapped by a cheap Brownie camera.
There follows a sequence of pictures
featuring GRANDPERE. The periods
are 1900, 1910, 1918--say in World War
I army uniform--1925, and the present.
The photographs in their mounting and
make-up, should suggest their separate
period flavors. The final photograph is
the exact pose we now see of GRAND-
PERE--his hand up, his arm waving.
[This can also be a spotlighted glimpse
of the actual actor as in previous
"pictures" of actual characters in the
play.] JACQUES speaks to the audience:)
There he is--my father--not as he was that night,
but many years before! Ah, the bon vivant! To
your good health, my friends! That was the first
picture I ever took--with a little Brownie box
camera. And that one--in his uniform--the whole
world was at war, but not with my father! And
here he is with my mother, when she went to
visit him at the barracks. And here he is in the
automobile he loved the best . . . the summer
his hair first started turning gray. And now tonight. This was the last picture of him I ever
took . . . the last . . .

(Gently, very gently.)
Hold it, old man--it is a time exposure!
(Wryly. Music can be heard in back
ground, playing "Hold! Hold! Hold!
Wait for Me!")
Ah, time! . . . The worst weather to be exposed
to.

(LOUIS and his family escort
GRANDPERE offstage, en route
home. LAURIE and JACQUES
also depart, leaving onstage only
PHILIPPE and BIBI.)
98

PHILIPPE
Come, Bibi--we go home.

BIBI
No--wait! I lied to him!

PHILIPPE
To whom, Bibi?

BIBI
Never mind. I'm going home.

PHILIPPE
Wait. You lied to Grandpere about what, Bibi?

(JACQUES hurries in to retrieve his camera.)

JACQUES
The old man must be feeling better. He is curs-
ing because Louis stole his naked pictures.

BIBI (quietly)
Uncle Louis didn't steal them. . . . I did.

PHILIPPE
You . . . took the pictures?

BIBI
Yes.

PHILIPPE
Why?

JACQUES
Why? Because he was angry! We did not sign
the paper--we failed him!

PHILIPPE
The pictures . . . what did you do with them?

BIBI
Nothing! I was so angry--I was----

PHILIPPE
What did you do? Answer me! What did you do
with the pictures?

BIBI
I tacked them up all over the school! In the school-
yard--in the hallways--everywhere!

PHILIPPE
Tomorrow morning you will go to the principal.
You will give him your apology. You will then
ask his permission to address the entire school--
in assembly. And you will make a public apology--
to everyone.

BIBI
Oh, no!

JACQUES
Philippe, you cannot do that!

PHILIPPE
He will do as I say!
        (PHILIPPE exits.)

BIBI
I--Uncle Jacques--when I get to school--and have
to climb up the steps in the auditorium--I will not
be able to do it! Please--Uncle Jacques--when
you go--take me with you!

JACQUES
Bibi--I can't take you with me!

BIBI
Please--you've got to! I cannot go to school
here any more! They will never let me alone

with their jokes!

JACQUES
Bibi--listen--you have to finish school--you have
to graduate--and go to the university and be a man
of importance!

BIBI
You didn't go to the university. Aren't you a man
of importance?

JACQUES
No--I don't know--It does not matter about me!

BIBI
It doesn't have to be forever, Uncle Jacques!
Just a little while--a few months, maybe. If
you don't want me with you any more, you can
send me back home!

JACQUES
Yes . . . it doesn't have to be forever.

BIBI
Will you, Uncle Jacques--will you? Please?

JACQUES
For a short time, maybe--why not? I could take
you everywhere! I would not have to go alone! Why
the hell do I have to see the Taj Mahal all by myself; I can see it with somebody! I tell you, boy--
the first time you see a bullfight in Madrid I am
going to take your picture! Yes! Now you get
through the day! Go to school! And when you
walk up the steps of the auditorium, you tell them
you are sorry. Tell them you do not want to be
a child and you do not yet know how to be a man--
and so you have done a foolish thing. And tomorrow you will be with me!--with me, Bibi!

(During the last, the BOYS have gone into position on
    one side of the stage. They are lined up in ranks
    to hear an announcement. The streamer and party
    props are pulled up, or off.)

BIBI (from C)
    Mr. Principal--Members of the Faculty--Fellow
    Students----
        (The voice fades, but he pantomimes the speech
        while the lights on him and the boys dim and
        come up on JACQUES. Now JACQUES comes
        down to the audience and speaks:)

JACQUES (with unabated excitement)
    Yes! I told him yes! And suddenly I was so ex-
    cited about it--so happy! Somebody with me--
    somebody from my own family--from home--my
    own godson! Already I was beginning to think of
    him as more than a godson! My own son! Why
    not? I understood him far better than his father
    did!

LAURIE (out of the shadows)
    Philippe is right.

JACQUES
    Philippe is wrong.

LAURIE
    What would you do if he were your son?

JACQUES
    Nothing!

LAURIE (shocked)
    Nothing?

JACQUES
    Damn it, Laurie--to make such a cause celebre
    of it! An apology, yes--to the principal only!
    But not to everyone!

102

LAURIE

It was an offense against everyone, was it not?

JACQUES

Offense? It was only a little prank--a joke! One of those funny things that makes one to cry! A foolishness, yes! But a child has a right to be a fool!

LAURIE

But nobody has a right to be a child--not forever, Jacques!

JACQUES (an instant)

You . . . mean me.

LAURIE

Well, you don't behave like a grown-up, responsible man, do you?

JACQUES (angry)

Responsible to what?

LAURIE (equally angry)

Ask Philippe! If you live in a family, you have to be responsible to it! If you go to a school-- responsible to it! If you live in St. Pierre----

JACQUES

I don't want to live in St. Pierre! And Bibi doesn't want to, either! And when I go, I'm going to take him with me!

LAURIE

No! You wouldn't do that!

JACQUES

Yes, I will! What is St. Pierre!

LAURIE

So . . . after all . . . you don't want to stay.
You don't want to live somewhere--you want to
live everywhere. You want to photograph every-
thing--and see nothing.

JACQUES

If you mean I see differently than you do--yes,
it's true!

(SONG: "SEEING THINGS.")

JACQUES (singing)

WE SEE A CHILD EATING ICE CREAM,
RIGHT THERE BEFORE US HE STANDS.
I SAY, "LOOK, WHAT A HAPPY FACE"
YOU SAY, "LOOK, HE'S GOT DIRTY HANDS".

WE SEE A CHILD IN A MAPLE TREE,
WE'RE WATCHING HIM CLIMB, YOU AND I.
YOU SAY, "COME DOWN, OR YOU'LL HURT
  YOURSELF"
I SAY, "GO UP, YOU'RE TOUCHING THE SKY."

THERE'S THE DIFFERENCE BETWEEN US
NO OBSERVER COULD MISS.
WHAT'S THE DIFFERENCE BETWEEN US?
ONLY THIS . . .

SEEING THINGS,
THERE'S A WAY OF SEEING THINGS,
A CERTAIN WAY OF SEEING THINGS
THAT MAKES THE DIFFERENCE.

IS THAT SUN UP THERE
A CIRCLE SPUN OF LIGHT AND AIR
OR JUST AN EVERYDAY, PRACTICAL SUN?

YOU AND I
HAVE A WAY OF SEEING THINGS,
A DIFFERENT WAY OF SEEING THINGS, I'D
  SAY

PAINT YOUR TRUTH WITH MY ILLUSION
PLEASE CONSIDER SEEING THINGS MY WAY.

LAURIE
    ATTRACTIVE AND CHARMING
    FOREVER IT SEEMS,
    DISTURBING, DISARMING
    MY SPINNER OF DREAMS.

    BUT DIFFERENT WE ARE
    AND DIFFERENT WE'LL STAY,
    TRY AS WE MIGHT
    WE WON'T FIND A WAY.

    I'M OF EARTH AND YOU'RE OF SKY,
    I LOVE YOU VERY MUCH
    I LOVE YOU VERY MUCH.
    GOOD-BY.

    SEEING THINGS,
    THERE'S A WAY OF SEEING THINGS,
    A CERTAIN WAY OF SEEING THINGS
    THAT MAKES THE DIFFERENCE.

    I NEED MORE THAN LOVE
    A SOMEONE TO BE CERTAIN OF,
    WHEN I REACH FOR HIM, HE MUST BE THERE.

JACQUES and LAURIE
    YOU AND I
    HAVE A WAY OF SEEING THINGS,
    A DIFFERENT WAY OF SEEING THINGS, I'D
      SAY.

ONE IS TRUTH AND ONE'S ILLUSION.

LAURIE
I'M OF EARTH AND YOU'RE OF SKY.

JACQUES
BUT I LOVE YOU VERY MUCH.

LAURIE
AND I LOVE YOU VERY MUCH.
GOOD-BY.

(The song concludes. The light fades on JACQUES
and LAURIE and comes up again, fully, on BIBI,
who is concluding his apology to the school.)

BIBI
So . . . as my uncle says . . . if I'm not a
child . . . and not a man . . . then I don't
know how to be! So I did something foolish . . .
and I am very sorry . . .
(He gets down off the auditorium
platform.)

BOY
Hey, Bibi--got anymore naked pictures?
BIBI
No, I haven't!
BOY
I'll give you my hockey stick for three of them!

OTHER BOYS
Me, too! I'll help you with your math test! . . .
etc., etc.

BIBI
I don't have them! Ganache got them!
106

GANACHE
  I did not!

BIBI
  Yes, you did! You took them out of the principal's
  office! Now you give them back! Before I go
  away, I have to return them to my grandfather!
  Hand them over!

  (GILLIE, NANETTE and ANNABELLE enter.)

GANACHE
  You want another fight?

BIBI
  You bet I do!

GILLIE
  Wait! I've got them!

BIBI
  Well, where are they?

GANACHE
  Come on, Gillie.

BOY
  How about it, Gillie?

(The ballet sequence begins. The dancers keep the
  pictures from BIBI by passing them from one
  to another as they perform an increasingly rit-
  ualistic chase. A platform or other device with
  a ramp, used in the staging, will add further
  dimensional variety to the dance. Directions
  for the actual dance sequence as performed in
  the Broadway show are given in the back of the
  book.)

(GILLIE dances around BIBI, exits upstage. BOYS
  pace around each other and exit, leaving BIBI,
  FOUFIE, NANETTE and ANNABELLE on stage.)

(GILLIE re-enters.)

BIBI

    Gillie Bonnard, come back here! Where are
those pictures?

(GILLIE dances around BIBI, getting pictures from
    FOUFIE. DANCERS enter and dance continues.
    GANACHE takes pictures from envelope, dropping
    envelope. GANACHE teases BIBI with pictures,
    then throws them in air. Pictures float to floor.
    All, disgusted, leave stage, including GANACHE.
    GILLIE, FOUFIE and BIBI pick up pictures.
    GILLIE gives pictures to BIBI. GILLIE exits.
    FOUFIE picks up envelope; gives to BIBI; starts
    to leave; comes back to look at pictures, then
    leaves. FOUFIE exits. BIBI goes down stairs--
    lead-in to GRANDPERE'S bedroom.)

(End of BALLET.)

GRANDPERE (wearing a smoking jacket and seating
    himself in an arm chair)
    Look at them! What happened to my pictures?
Torn--dirty! Look at this one! She was carry-
ing a flag! Where is her flag?... And this one--
what are all these little pin holes?

BIBI

    The boys were throwing darts at her.

GRANDPERE

    Quel sacrilege! Someone had a very good aim!

BIBI

    I'm sorry, Grandpere.

108

(He starts to go.)

GRANDPERE
    One moment! Not so fast, monsieur! One of
    them is missing!

BIBI
    Ah, you're wrong. They're all there!

GRANDPERE
    Do not tell me, my young boulevardier! Where
    is the girl who is wearing that little lacy nothing?

BIBI
    She's there! I know she's there! I saw her only
    a moment ago! . . . There! There she is!

GRANDPERE
    Ah, yes, here she is! Very polite, very modest.
    Peekaboo!
        (He offers BIBI candy.)
    Here--have one. These are plain--the dark ones
    have brandy centers.

BIBI
    Brandy, please.

GRANDPERE
    Yes, I too prefer brandy.
        (BIBI helps himself.)
    This one is my favorite. Every time I look at
    her I'm afraid I will get arrested.

BIBI
    It is because she is wearing something.

GRANDPERE
    You have made a very delicate point! Have another
    brandy! But there is a slight--an almost imper-

ceptible fault in this picture!

BIBI
A fault?

GRANDPERE
I think the way she holds her arms--like this!
Study me now. Study me closely. What do you
see?

BIBI
I see nothing wrong, Grandpere.

GRANDPERE
Nothing? Look at me with the careful eye.
Now suppose--just suppose--I hold my arms--
voilà --like this! Better--no?

BIBI
Well, it is somewhat better, Grandpere.

GRANDPERE
Aha!

BIBI
But----

GRANDPERE
What is the "but"?

BIBI
Look--if she is the way you are--in your posi-
tion--then you will not be able to see this beautiful part of the lady!

GRANDPERE
Have a double brandy!

(JACQUES appears. He carries a suitcase. He
looks at it; debates whether to take it into his

110

father's room; decides to leave it outside,
then calls, as he enters:)

JACQUES
Bibi! Bibi! Eh, Papa--are you getting him
drunk on chocolates?
(Reaching to the floor, he picks
up a scrap.)
Here, what is this?

GRANDPERE
Well, what is it?

JACQUES
Looks like a flag.
(Looks at the pictures.)
Ah, Papa--how lucky you are! So many ladies--
and none of them gives you any trouble.

GRANDPERE
You know why I have so many of them? Because
I do not have one. A long time ago I had one girl
--and I married her. Only one--and I didn't need
any of these . . . How many girls do you have,
Bibi?

BIBI
Oh, there's Gillie and Nanette and Annabelle.

GRANDPERE (to JACQUES)
And you? . . . How many girls have you got?

JACQUES (lightly, as usual)
Me? I've got a thousand of them!

GRANDPERE
You do not even have one! I hear you and
Laurie are no more!

JACQUES
Yes . . . it's over. Papa, don't worry about
me!

GRANDPERE
You have walnuts in your head! . . . Of course I
worry about you! Why don't you get married?

JACQUES
Oh, I will, Papa!

(MUSIC begins to play in background.)

JACQUES
I will get married and have a son and I will name
him Alexandre, after you--and he will be born
with a white mustache!

GRANDPERE
You will get married? To whom? A thousand
girls?

JACQUES
Yes!

GRANDPERE
A thousand girls are not so many as one! As
you will find out one day!

(SONG: "A CERTAIN GIRL":)

GRANDPERE
A CERTAIN GIRL,
SOME CERTAIN GIRL,
IS BOUND TO HAPPEN ALONG,
COME ALONG ONE WONDERFUL DAY.

YOU'll SEE HER SMILE,

SOME CERTAIN SMILE,
AND THAT WILL TICKLE YOU SO,
MAKE YOU GO AROUND IN THE DOPIEST WAY.

THOUGH YOU WERE FREE
AND HAPPY TO BE
SHE'LL COME ALONG
SWISHING HER SKIRT
WALKING A CERTAIN WALK.

THAT CERTAIN GIRL.
AND FROM THAT MOMENT ON,
YOU'RE TOTALLY THROUGH,
THERE'S NOTHING YOU CAN POSSIBLY DO
BUT SPEND YOUR LIFETIME WOOING A
    CERTAIN GIRL.

GRANDPERE
    A CERTAIN GIRL
    SOME CERTAIN GIRL,
    IS BOUND TO HAPPEN
       ALONG,
    COME ALONG ONE
       WONDERFUL DAY.

    YOU'LL SEE HER
       SMILE,
    SOME CERTAIN SMILE,
    AND THAT WILL TICKLE
       YOU SO,
    MAKE YOU GO AROUND
       IN THE MOPIEST WAY.

JACQUES and BIBI
    A CERTAIN GIRL
    SOME CERTAIN GIRL,

    ONE WONDERFUL DAY.

    YOU'LL SEE HER
       SMILE
    SOME CERTAIN SMILE

ALL
    THOUGH YOU WERE FREE
    AND HAPPY TO BE
    SHE'LL COME ALONG
113

GRANDPERE
     SWISHING HER SKIRT
     WALKING A CERTAIN WALK,
     THAT CERTAIN GIRL.

ALL
     AND FROM THAT MOMENT ON YOU'RE
       TOTALLY THROUGH,
     THERE'S NOTHING YOU CAN POSSIBLY DO
     BUT SPEND YOUR LIFETIME WOOING A
       CERTAIN . . .

GRANDPERE
     A CERTAIN GIRL

JACQUES
     . . . A CERTAIN GIRL

BIBI
          . . . A CERTAIN GIRL

GRANDPERE
     SOME CERTAIN GIRL

JACQUES
     . . . SOME CERTAIN GIRL

BIBI
          . . . SOME CERTAIN GIRL

ALL
     IS BOUND TO HAPPEN ALONG,
     COME ALONG ONE WONDERFUL DAY.

GRANDPERE
     YOU'LL SEE HER SMILE

JACQUES
     . . . YOU'LL SEE HER SMILE

BIBI
     . . . YOU'LL SEE HER SMILE

GRANDPERE
  SOME CERTAIN SMILE

JACQUES
  . . . SOME CERTAIN SMILE

BIBI
     . . . SOME CERTAIN SMILE

ALL
  AND THAT WILL TICKLE YOU SO,
  MAKE YOU GO AROUND IN THE DOPIEST WAY.

  THOUGH YOU WERE FREE
  AND HAPPY TO BE
  SHE'LL COME ALONG

GRANDPERE
  SWISHING HER

JACQUES
  . . . SWISHING HER

BIBI
     . . . SWISHING HER

ALL
  SKIRT!
  WALKING A CERTAIN

GRANDPERE
  WALK!

JACQUES
  . . . A CERTAIN WALK

BIBI

. . . A CERTAIN WALK

GRANDPERE
THAT CERTAIN GIRL

JACQUES
. . . THAT CERTAIN GIRL

BIBI

. . . THAT CERTAIN GIRL

ALL
AND FROM THAT MOMENT ON YOU FLY LIKE
A DOVE,
THERE'S NOTHING YOU'RE INCAPABLE OF,
BECAUSE YOU'RE LIVING, LOVING A CERTAIN
BECAUSE YOU'RE LIVING, LOVING A CERTAIN
BECAUSE YOU'RE LIVING, LOVING A CERTAIN
GIRL!
(Applause, applause, applause!)

ALL

(Encore)
A CERTAIN GIRL,
SOME CERTAIN GIRL,
IS BOUND TO HAPPEN ALONG
COME ALONG ONE WONDERFUL DAY . . .
AY . . . AY . . . AY

YOU'LL SEE HER SMI . . . I . . . I . . . ILE
SOME CERTAIN SMI . . . I . . . I . . . ILE
AND THAT WILL TICKLE YOU SO,
MAKE YOU GO AROUND IN THE DOPIEST
WAY . . .
(Directly after "A CERTAIN GIRL", BIBI
says, with happy impulsiveness:)
BIBI
Grandpere! You come with us!

116

GRANDPERE (eagerly--always delighted to go any-
    where)
    Go with you? Certainly! Where? The Six
    Angels? A little allez-oop!

BIBI
    Tell him, Uncle Jacques.

JACQUES (quietly, to BIBI)
    Bibi, he could not come with us.

GRANDPERE
    Of course I can come! Why not? Where?

JACQUES
    Papa, I am leaving tonight . . . and taking Bibi
    with me.

GRANDPERE
    Taking him where? You mean London . . .
    Paris . . . everywhere?

JACQUES
    Yes.

GRANDPERE
    You cannot mean this seriously?

JACQUES
    Not too seriously, I hope. With a smile.

GRANDPERE (wryly)
    With a smile, eh? Will his mother smile? And
    his father? Will they smile and say "cheese"?

JACQUES (an outburst--but still keeping his good
    humor)
    Papa, listen! You don't think I would take him
    away without their permission? And why shouldn't

117

they give it? I won't take him away forever!
Six months--maybe a year!

GRANDPERE
To do what?

JACQUES
See the world! He is old enough to start enjoying
the world!

GRANDPERE (with a wry wink, to BIBI)
He always talks about "the world" as if we are
not in it. All the happiness is--**out** there!
      (To JACQUES, hiding his feelings with
      a smile.)
It may come as a surprise to you, but I have
heard this boy laugh--in St. Pierre! Even when
you were not at home!

JACQUES
Come, Bibi--we will talk to your father.

GRANDPERE (his first angry outburst)
No! You will not again put Philippe in the position of having to say no to the boy!

JACQUES (also angry)
For God's sake, why should he say no?

GRANDPERE (smiling again)
What a charming thief you are, Jacques!

JACQUES
Thief?

GRANDPERE
I have been calling Louis a thief--and he never
stole anything. You are the thief of the family.

118

JACQUES
   Why? What have I stolen?

GRANDPERE
   Affection you did not work for--as Philippe has
   worked. The daily slavery of bringing up children.
   "Did you brush your teeth? Are you telling the
   truth?" The same rules that make a father the
   hated monster of the house--so that a self-centered
   little animal may turn into the fine boy that Bibi
   is! . . . and when the job is nearly finished you
   would steal him away!

JACQUES
   No, Papa, I will not steal him away. Bibi--
   come on!

GRANDPERE (angry now)
   No! I said wait! Before you go, let him know
   what you are doing here in St. Pierre!

JACQUES
   Papa, what has that got to do with this?

GRANDPERE (to BIBI)
   He is taking pictures of us and he will sell them
   to a magazine! He is selling us, Bibi! He does
   not care about people, only pictures of us! Hold
   it!

JACQUES (quietly)
   That's not true, Papa!

GRANDPERE
   Then tell him what is true!

JACQUES
   I have never lied to him!

GRANDPERE

No? He thinks you are the happiest man in the world!

JACQUES

That is not far from the truth!

GRANDPERE

Then what do you need him for? What do you need any of us for? You have a lot of cameras and quite a few prizes and every hotel manager in the world knows you! But you are so alone! You do not have a son like Bibi! You did not come home to take pictures--you came home to be <u>home</u>! And now you want to take some of that home away with you! You cannot do that, Jacques! You have to make your own home! <u>Somewhere,</u> Jacques--somewhere in the world!

JACQUES

You don't understand me, Papa! I have everything I want!

GRANDPERE

You have <u>nothing</u> that you want! Tell him!

JACQUES (suddenly turning to BIBI; his last brave bluff falling apart)

Bibi--you listen to me--what I have----Prizes, Bibi--I will show you a dozen prizes! And everywhere in the world--friends--people I know--they call me by my name. I have--what I have, Bibi-- what I have----

(An instant. He cannot go on with it. He says, quietly.)

. . . nothing, Bibi.

BIBI

No--Uncle Jacques--don't say that!

120

JACQUES

No, he's right. Nothing . . . I have acquaintances,
Bibi--no friends--and when they meet me they say,
"This is Jacques--uh--I have forgotten his last
name!"
(A little outcry.)
Bonnard! My friend of the family Bonnard! . . .
He was right--I was not taking you away for your
sake--only for my own!

BIBI

Then I'll go for your sake!

JACQUES

No!

BIBI

Uncle Jacques! Please!

JACQUES

No! If you come with me you will see me as I am--
running from one empty hotel room to another!

BIBI

Please, Uncle Jacques!

JACQUES (it tears out of him)

No! I don't want you with me!

BIBI

You do--yes, you do!

JACQUES

Yes--today! Today I do! But tomorrow I will be
on a job and you will be a nuisance to me! He was
right--I do not care about people, only pictures!

BIBI

No! I don't believe that! It's not true!

JACQUES
I'll show you. I want a picture of the way you
are right now.
    (He grabs Bibi's camera.)

BIBI
No! Please don't take my picture now!

JACQUES
Just as you are! No, don't wipe the tears away!
Hold it!

BIBI
Stop it! Stop it!

JACQUES
The perfect picture! Perfect!

BIBI
No--please--please----
    (BIBI leaves. GRANDPERE comes out
    of the darkness where he has been during
    the last few speeches.)

GRANDPERE
You did that very well.

JACQUES
What did you say?

GRANDPERE
I said you did that very well.

JACQUES
Thank you, Papa . . . I came to take pictures of
St. Pierre . . . and I take a picture of myself.

GRANDPERE
Will it be a good one?

JACQUES (with a gentle laugh)
    Not perfect, I'm sure. . . . I'll know when it
    develops.

GRANDPERE
    Oh, I would like to see that!

JACQUES
    I'll bring it to you, Papa. In person.

GRANDPERE
    And now, my son, you must go.

JACQUES (quietly, with a sad smile)
    Go? But how can I leave you? You are a sick
    man!

GRANDPERE
    No, monsieur, not me! I am like a winter wine.
    If I have lasted this long, through the cold, I will
    only get better as I get older!
        (Then, with a wry smile.)
    . . . Anyway, let us say . . . that this is so.

JACQUES
    Yes, Papa, let us say it is so.

GRANDPERE
    Yes . . .
        (Then, quietly, painfully, but trying
        to smile.)
    Good-by, my idiot . . . My dear, dear idiot . . .
    good-by.

JACQUES
    Good-by, Papa.
        (They embrace. It is GRANDPERE
        who breaks away first, lest he weep.
        He moves back into the darkness. The
123

　　　　light on him is fading fast.)
Papa, good-by! Say it once again, Papa! Say
something again! *Au'voir*, Papa--*Au'voir!Au'voir!*
　　　　(As always, too late. GRANDPERE'S
　　　　light is out. Remorse and Regret, the
　　　　twin despairs of the past, are plain on
　　　　JACQUES' face. And now, slowly, all
　　　　the physical aspects of the stage seem
　　　　to disappear, leaving JACQUES alone
　　　　and naked, forlorn in memory.)

JACQUES
　　　　Yes, the memory plays tricks. I sometimes
　　　　wonder if I really had that last conversation
　　　　with him. If only I had a picture of that moment!
　　　　Of all the times not to have taken a picture of
　　　　him----It was the last good-by. The old roué,
　　　　the old goat, the old beloved bastard! He was
　　　　not faking after all! He died in the night.

(Bibi's graduation. The boys of the GLEE CLUB
　　　　enter.)

　　　　　　(SONG: "ST. PIERRE" [REPRISE])

ALL BOYS
　　　　AU-DESSUS DES COLLINES DE ST. PIERRE,
　　　　LES VENTS SOUFFLENT TOUTES LES NUAGES
　　　　FAISANT CHAQUE JOUR UN JOUR CLAIR.

　　　　ST. PIERRE!
　　　　ST. PIERRE!
　　　　MA MAISON,
　　　　MON VILLAGE,
　　　　MON PAYS,
　　　　JE REVOIS!
　　　　　　(As "ST. PIERRE" builds in volume,
　　　　　　　　　　　124

                    JACQUES steps forward.   At the con-
                    clusion of the music:)

JACQUES (to the audience)
        Yes, many years have passed since Bibi's gradu-
        ation day.   And, you know, of all the prizes that
        I have won since then, none can compare with the
        one my father gave to me when he said, "You did
        that very well, my son," and I'm going to pass it
        on to my own son, Alexandre, who is named after
        his grandfather and was born seven days after the
        flood.   So let us remember them. . . .

        (SONG: "THE HAPPY TIME" [REPRISE])

JACQUES (singing)
        THE REASON I TOLD YOU THAT IS THIS:
        I'M LONGING TO SEE YOU SMILE AND HEAR
          YOU LAUGH
        SO I CAN HAVE THE PHOTOGRAPH
        AND REMEMBER YOU
        REMEMBERING
        THE HAPPY TIME!

                        CURTAIN

PROPERTIES

GENERAL

ACT ONE:

Photographer's Studio: Projection screen, light stands or spotlight, pedestal, vase, rose, camera tripod, lights, and other photographic equipment. *[If film is not used, need following items: Rose, birthday cake with candles, boy's kite, many roses and other flowers.]* Bonnard Home: Dining table, chairs, stools, dinner settings for nine people (napkins, glasses, silver, etc.) Theatre: Folding Screen with clothing for The Six Angels, bench. Bedroom: Two small beds, window, bench. School yard: Jungle Jim.

ACT TWO:

Studio: Red darkroom light, camera, table with films in hypo baths, etc. Gymnasium: Piano, ladder, party decorations (crepe paper streamers, etc.), wine bottle and glass. School: Folding chairs, auditorium platform with steps. School yard: Jungle Jim. Grandpere's Room: Easy chair, scrap of paper on floor.

PERSONAL

ACT ONE:

PHILLIPE: Large pocket watch with chain.
GRANDPERE: Flower, handkerchief.
JACQUES: Small camera, pen.
BIBI: Pajamas, hard-boiled egg, note.

ACT TWO:

JACQUES: Rubbergloves, opened telegrams, fancy box containing mementoes, camera, suitcase.
BIBI: Tyrolean hat, camera.
GRANDPERE: Box of chocolates.
GILLIE: Pictures in envelope.
LOUIS, PHILIPPE, SUZANNE, FELICE, NA-NETTE, GILLIE and ANNABELLE: Black balloons.

126

In addition to the preceding items, the following articles were used in the Broadway show.

ACT ONE – STAGE PRESET

pink, yellow, and orange bouquet of flowers
paper sunflower
2 candlesticks
wine bottle with corkscrew
5 champagne glasses
dressing table
2 stools
2 folding chairs
wicker furniture (2 cushioned armchairs, 3 stools,
  4 straight chairs)
extra envelope with pictures
pin
stool under dressing room

ACT TWO – STAGE PRESET

high stool
3 wicker stools (off right)
6 pictures for boys
wicker armchair with cushion
2 folding chairs and step

OTHER PROPERTIES (offstage)

3 wicker stools (Act One)
9 wooden stools (Act One)
floral centerpiece (Act One)
sheet of paper in envelope (Act One)
mixing bowl & beater (Act Two)
3 drums   )
6 drumsticks) both acts

OTHER PROPERTIES (offstage)

soup tureen with cover and ladle (Act One)
wooden salad bowl with fork and spoon (Act One)
floral cushion (Act Two)
stacks of 8 x 10 (one sealed, one opened & face to face)
fruit bowl with practical fruit (oranges, apples, bananas, and grapes)
vase and milk pitcher
paring knife in fruit bowl
tray with 6 cups & saucers, cream pitcher, milk pitcher and coffee urn
bouquet of yellow & purple flowers
high painted stool

PERSONAL PROPS

Philippe — eye glasses

Grandpere — cigar, comb

Suzanne — apron, table cloth

BALLET SEQUENCE
for Act II (pages 107-108)

1. GILLIE dances around BIBI, exits upstage.

2. BOYS pace around each other and exit, leaving BIBI, FOUFIE, NANETTE and ANNABELLE on stage.

3. (GILLIE re-enters.)

BIBI (spoken)
Gillie Bonnard, come back here! Where are those pictures?

4. GILLIE dances around BIBI, getting pictures from FOUFIE, and begins new downbeat of dance at BIBI, as she does turn to floor.

5. Entrance of DANCER #1.

6. GILLIE gives pictures to FOUFIE.

7. DANCER #2 gets pictures from FOUFIE and goes to TEARDROP, giving pictures to NANETTE.

8. NANETTE leaves TEARDROP with pictures; goes into spin with DANCER #1. GANACHE gets pictures from DANCER #1.

9. GANACHE leaps with DANCER #2; circles left behind platform and up platform to begin "Keep Away."

10. ALL BOYS on stage. GANACHE tosses to DANCER #3, DANCER #3 to DANCER #2, DANCER #2 to DANCER #3.

11. DANCER #3 hands pictures to ANNA-
    BELLE, but keeps up motion of "Keep
    Away."

12. ANNABELLE crosses lip stage L to
    stage R with pictures. NANETTE stops
    her, with GILLIE, stage R for:

13. "NANETTE'S Blush"--All freeze
    (Count 6)

14. GIRLS break, run across lip to TEAR-
    DROP. Up TEARDROP, then follow-up
    of leap off TEARDROP. GILLIE first,
    NANETTE second, ANNABELLE last.
    [During girls' circling on TEARDROP
    NANETTE gives pictures to GILLIE.]

15. "M & G Drop"--GILLIE and GANACHE.
    DANCER #4 circles from ramp to be-
    tween NANETTE and DANCER #2.
    (Freeze for a moment--count 13)

16. DANCER #4 takes pictures from GILLIE
    and gives them to GANACHE.

17. GANACHE circles L. He and DANCER
    #5 do leap; Circle left. DANCER #5 exits.
    GANACHE "hiddenly" gives pictures to
    DANCER #4. All exit, except GILLIE,
    NANETTE, ANNABELLE, GANACHE,
    DANCER #4 and BIBI. Enter FOUFIE.

18. Business about where are pictures.
    GILLIE exits R. GANACHE and BIBI
    follow. DANCER #4 walks to trapdoor L
    and sits.

19. FOUFIE--"Psst"--points to DANCER #4,
    showing NANETTE.

"ANITRA'S DANCE" (slow motion)

1. NANETTE at pole. Music starts when she steps off platform. She dances to DANCER #4 at L trapdoor.

2. NANETTE puts right foot on DANCER #4's shoulder, bending him down to his back, feet straight in air.

3. NANETTE takes pictures. Does turns to stage R--leading to "Release."

4. THREE GIRLS dance toward DANCER #4 in diagonal line.

5. DANCER #4 up from trapdoor, backs girls up.

6. NANETTE does slow turn.

7. DANCER #5 comes down ramp R--gets pictures from NANETTE, continuing L, gives pictures to DANCER #6 at Jungle Jim. (DANCER #6 switch in actual pack of pictures.)

8. DANCER #6 gives pictures to DANCER #7 on TEARDROP, who in turn gives pictures to DANCER #8 on TEARDROP. Simultaneously, GANACHE slides down pole.

THIS LEADS INTO NEW DOWNBEAT - BIBI:

1. BIBI enters L onto TEARDROP. Takes pictures from DANCER #8. He leaps onto stage, facing upstage, at GANACHE. (GANACHE upstage/BIBI downstage.)

131

2. BIBI runs up ramp to pole--leaps to
   behind pole--GANACHE does "Land
   Dive" on platform.

3. GANACHE chases BIBI in front of
   pole to upstage of platform.

4. BIBI up to platform--then off, and
   runs to TEARDROP.

5. GANACHE chases BIBI to TEARDROP--
   does slide--holding BIBI'S foot.

6. FOUFIE hits BIBI on foot. BIBI drops
   pictures.

7. DANCER #4 gets pictures from floor;
   runs to TEARDROP; does suspended
   jeté off TEARDROP to R to run at
   GANACHE.

8. "Rag Doll"--DANCER #4 jumps on
   GANACHE--GANACHE drops DANCER
   #4 down (Rag Doll), then throws him out
   R. DANCER #4 to floor.

9. BIBI gets pictures from DANCER #4,
   goes upstage just left of C, facing upstage.

10. GANACHE jumps over DANCER #4
    to BIBI; takes pictures from BIBI.

11. GANACHE circles down left in front
    of tear. DANCERS #5, #6 and #8 dive
    at GANACHE, landing flat on floor.

12. GANACHE up from behind on platform--
    down ramp to DL, facing upstage, to
    BIBI. GANACHE takes pictures from
    envelope, dropping envelope.

13. GANACHE teases BIBI with pictures, then throws them in air.

14. Pictures float to floor. All,disgusted, leave stage, including GANACHE.

15. GILLIE, FOUFIE and BIBI pick up pictures. GILLIE gives pictures to BIBI. GILLIE exits.
BIBI up ramp.
FOUFIE picks up envelope; goes up stairs; gives to BIBI; starts to leave; comes back to look at pictures. FOUFIE exits.

BIBI down stairs--lead-in to GRAND-PERE'S bedroom.

(End of BALLET.)